To Mike & Lisa

Chameleons in the Garden

Being Jackson's, Doing What Jackson's Do

Mary Lovein

Big Island of Hawaii

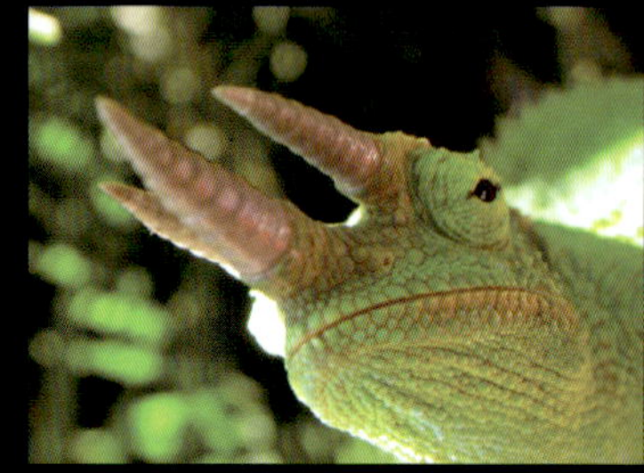

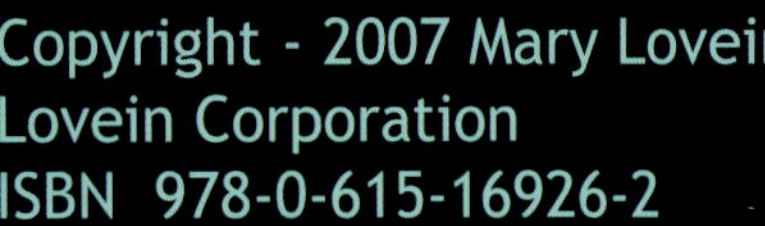

Copyright - 2007 Mary Lovein
Lovein Corporation
ISBN 978-0-615-16926-2

The author / photographer retains sole copyright
to all content in this book.

Wildlife - Jackson's Chameleons - Education
Reptiles - Photography - Gift - Lizards - Nature
Big Island of Hawaii - Environment
Coffee Table Book - Non-fiction

Editor, Karin Stanton
Technical Editor, Edward I. Pollak, Ph.D.
Design Consultant, Jerri Waterman

No reproductions are permitted without consent of the author
P.O. Box 773, Holualoa, HI, 96725

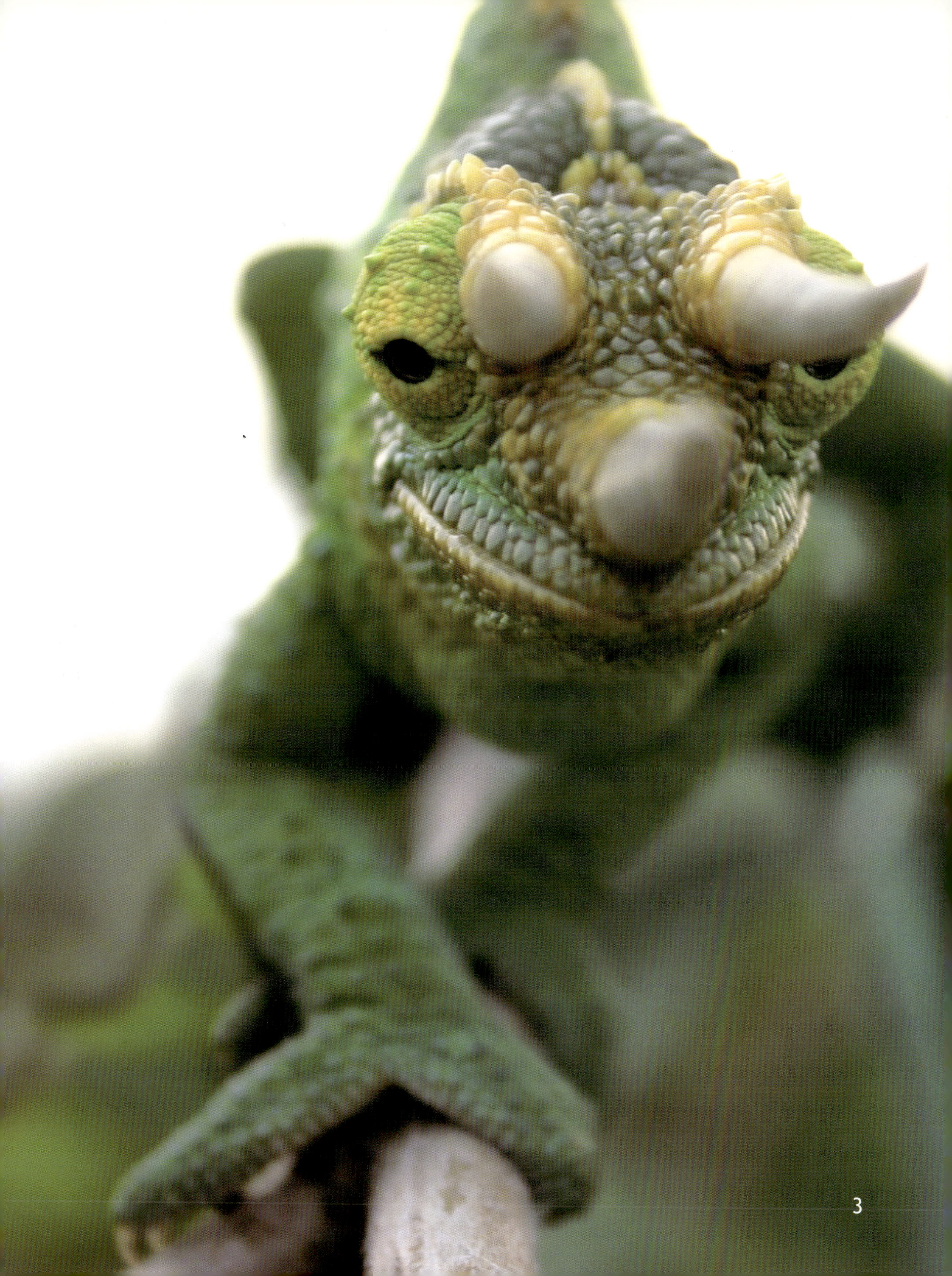

Artists Mary Lovein and her husband Matt Lovein
have opportunities to observe Jackson's chameleons daily,
while working in their open air studios.
he 1,500-foot elevation provides a good environment for the chameleons,
as well as the Loveins.

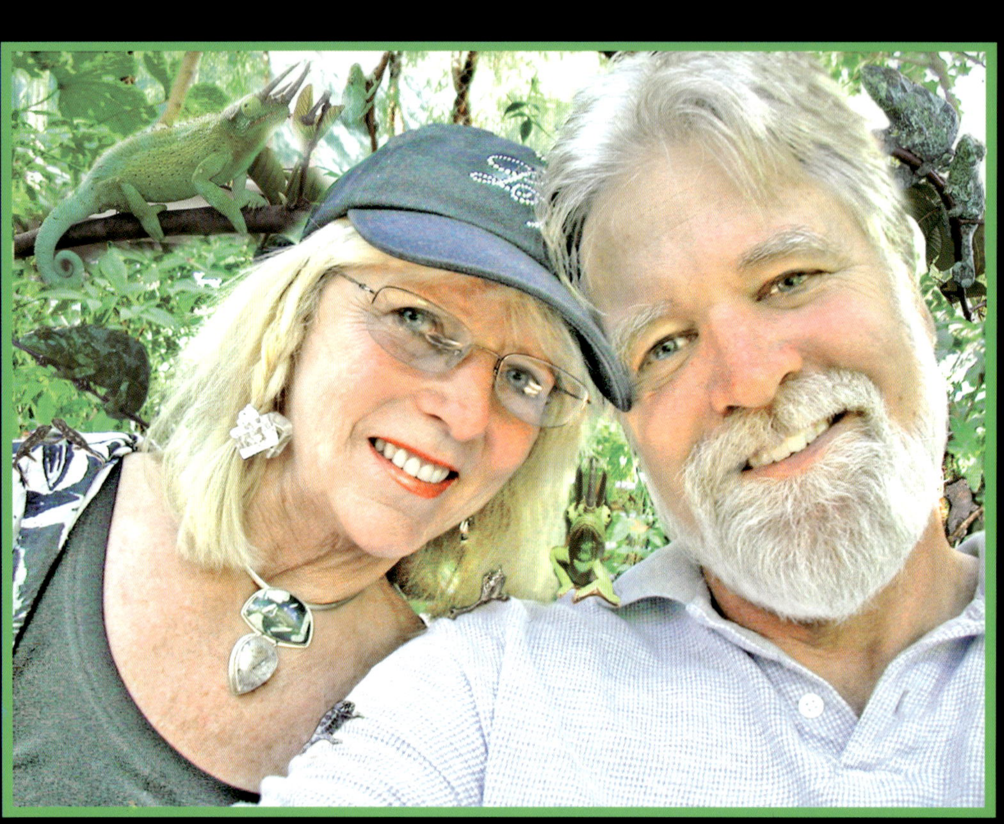

"As we look at each branch, the trees reveal glorious chameleons
going about their daily lives. It is somewhat expected,
but still surprising to see them in nature.

Together we document and discover
more about these very private and magical creatures.
The more we know, the more they remain
delightfully mysterious and fascinating."

Introduction

by Karin Stanton

Feeling the Love in 'Cham' Country

While coffee made its first appearance on the Big Island in the late 1820s and the banana was imported in the mid 1850s, the Jackson's chameleon was not introduced to Hawaii until the 1970s.

The owner of a pet store on Oahu, with a big idea and a valid permit to import the Jackson's chameleons, made a small but crucial mistake. Apparently, he released some into his backyard and intended to collect them after they became hydrated. He soon found out, chameleons are not so easily rediscovered once ensconced in Hawaii's tropical foliage.

After that accidental introduction, chameleons multiplied and caught on as something of a fad pet for a short time. Though remaining on the non-native wildlife list, they are an established species, blending into the lush landscape of this Pacific paradise. Jackson's chameleons have adapted and can be spotted by careful observers in forested areas up and down the island chain.

The home of Matt and Mary Lovein, in a private community on the slopes of Mount Hualalai, above Kailua-Kona is also known to some as The Lovein Lizard Spa. The Lovein's lanai offers a close up view of chameleon habitat. Family and friends delight in watching chameleons, which are hard to spot with untrained eyes.

The garden features palms, blossoms, banana plants, guava, avocado and silver oak trees, as well as "baby bushes" or chameleon nurseries. The home is built on post and pier, offering tree-top views at eye level, through every window and possible vantage point from the expansive lanai. "Look," Mary whispers, "We can spot five of them from here. Can you see them?"

To the uninitiated, it's typical tropical greenery, but as she begins pointing at them, the chameleons pop out of the landscape, a little like "Where's Waldo." Suddenly, the view of the Pacific Ocean, the seaside village that was a favorite of ancient royalty and the monster cruise ship in Kailua Bay don't seem nearly as captivating as seeing a chameleon hold on to a branch with his little toes.

"I feel so fortunate to see these living sculptures," Mary says. "From the first time I saw a chameleon, it was fascination that eventually turned into a lifestyle change, making a good life even better."

Acknowledgements

Matt Lovein for sharing the experience and his keen ability to spot chameleons.

Karin Stanton is a journalist in Kona who writes for Associated Press. When I told her my ideas for this project, she was immediately interested in participating.
Thank you, Karin, for your professional assistance and friendship.

Edward I. Pollak, Ph.D. is a fellow chameleon enthusiast who has been extremely supportive and encouraging.
I am grateful for the corrections and suggestions.
Dr. Pollak is a professor of animal behavior and biopsychology in the Department of Psychology at West Chester University of Pennsylvania.

Jerri Waterman is a graphic artist who offered to share her technical expertise and knowledge of Adobe InDesign software used to create this book. Thank you Jerri, for coaching me and for your patience and sense of humor.

Penmar Hawaii specializes in project management of book publishing.
I wish to thank Amy Yamamoto for providing me with printing guidelines.

Norm & Ann Goody of Three Ring Ranch in Kona
http://www.threeringranch.org

CHAMELEONS! Online E-Zine
http://www.chameleonnews.com

Thank you to all those not mentioned, who have appreciated my pictures and encouraged me to publish a book about chameleons, wild in Hawaii.

Mary

Enjoy the journey
as you discover more
about these amazing creatures
and
awaken to the glory
of their quiet world.

This book will give you
a glimpse into
the life of chameleons
in Hawaii,
where they adorn the
trees like ornaments in
a surrealistic dream.

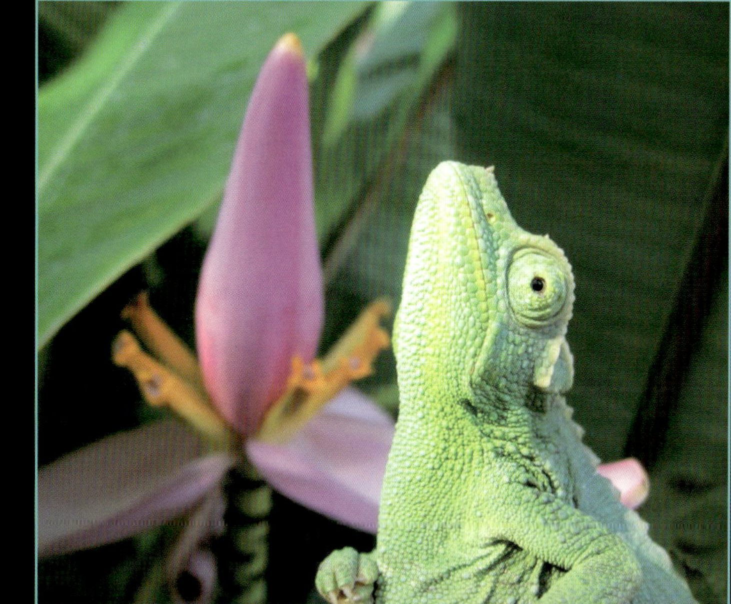

Jackson's chameleons
were named after
Sir Frederick Jackson (1860-1938),
a British explorer
who became governor of Uganda.

Jackson's chameleons
were imported to Hawaii in 1972
and now are an established species.

Hawaii is one of the few places on the planet
where they are found in natural habitat,
other than their place of origin,
Mt. Kenya, Africa.

The scientific name is
Chamaeleo (Trioceros) jacksonii xantholophus,
which is a subspecies of
C. jacksonii.

The chameleons comprise
a highly distinctive family
(Chamaeleonidae)
within the suborder of lizards
(Sauria)
and the class
Reptilia.

Why is this Woman Smiling?

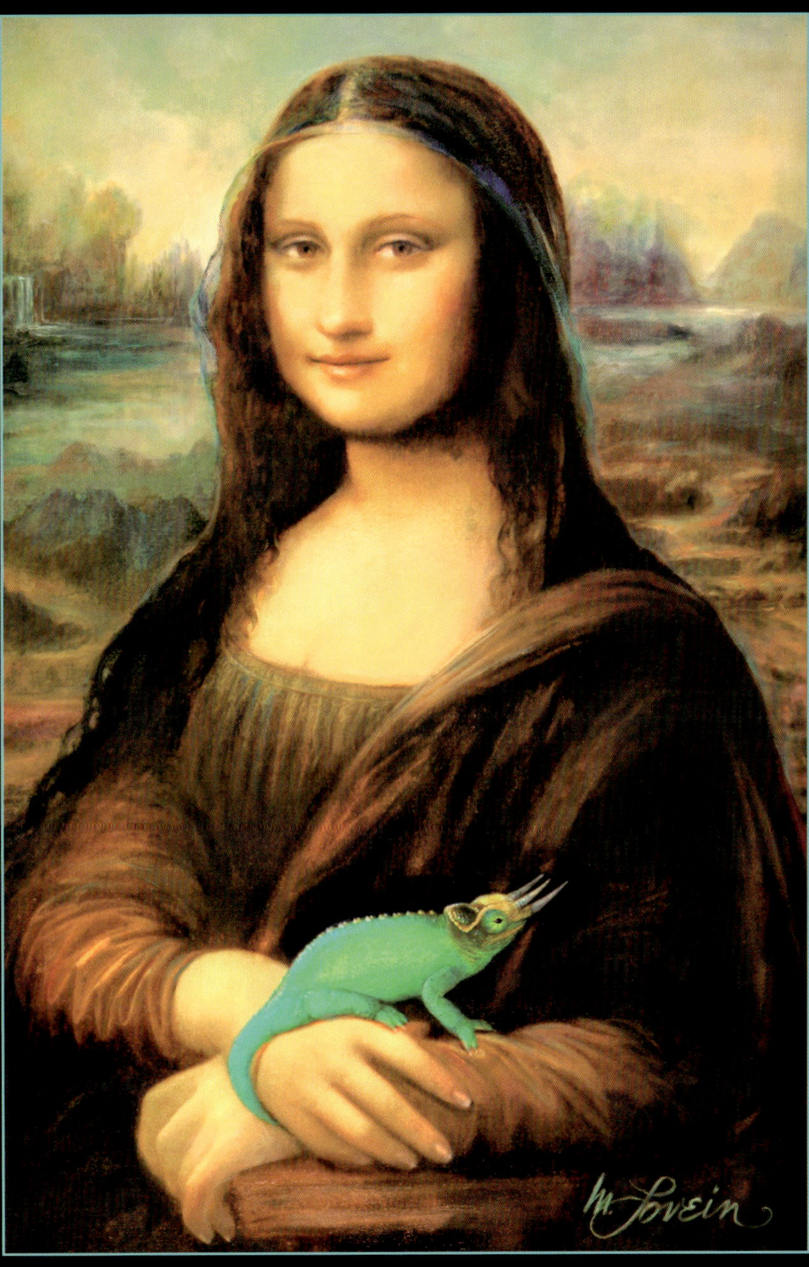

Acrylic Painting on Canvas

View from the Mountain

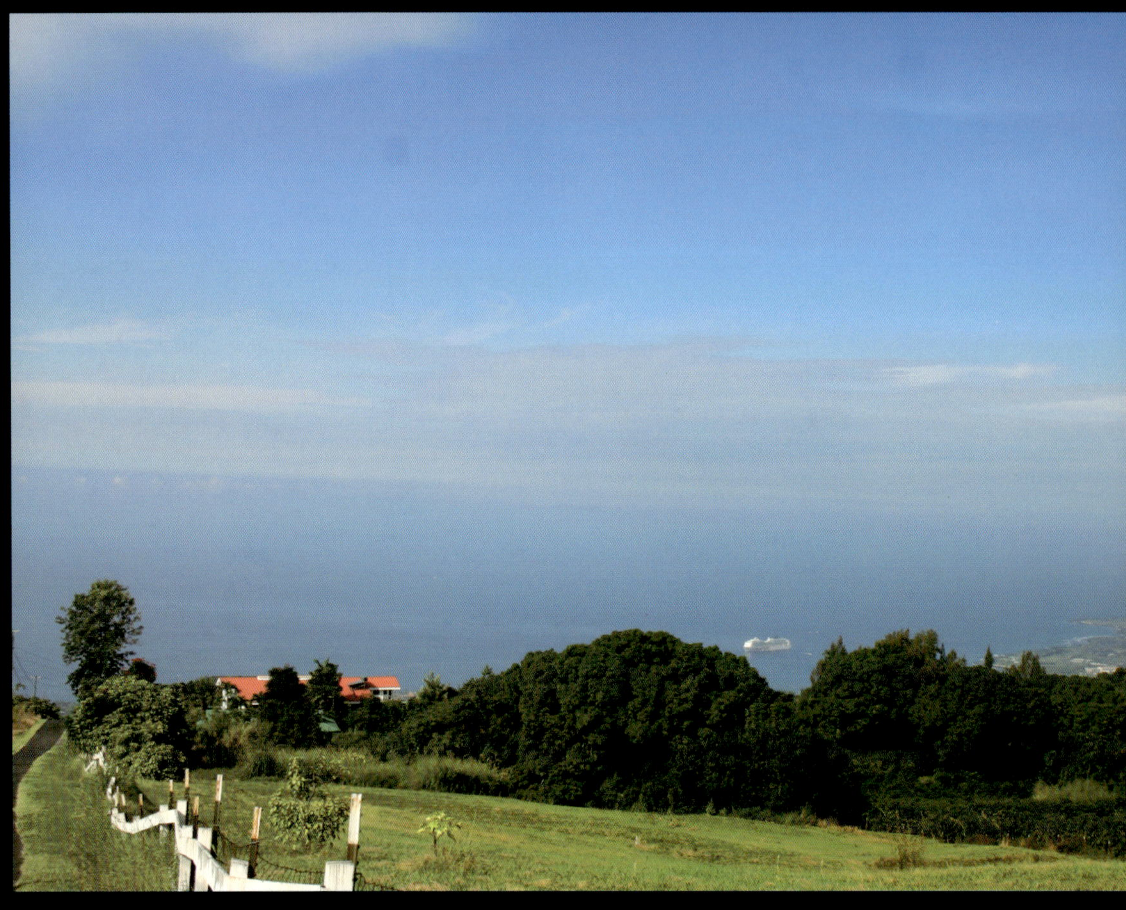

Our house is surrounded by a variety of trees including some chameleon favorites: coffee, Christmas berry, avocado, silver oak, guava, macadamia nut and mango. Morning sun and frequent afternoon showers provide almost idyllic conditions for the Jackson's chameleons, on the slopes of Mount Hualalai, one of the Big Island's five volcanoes.

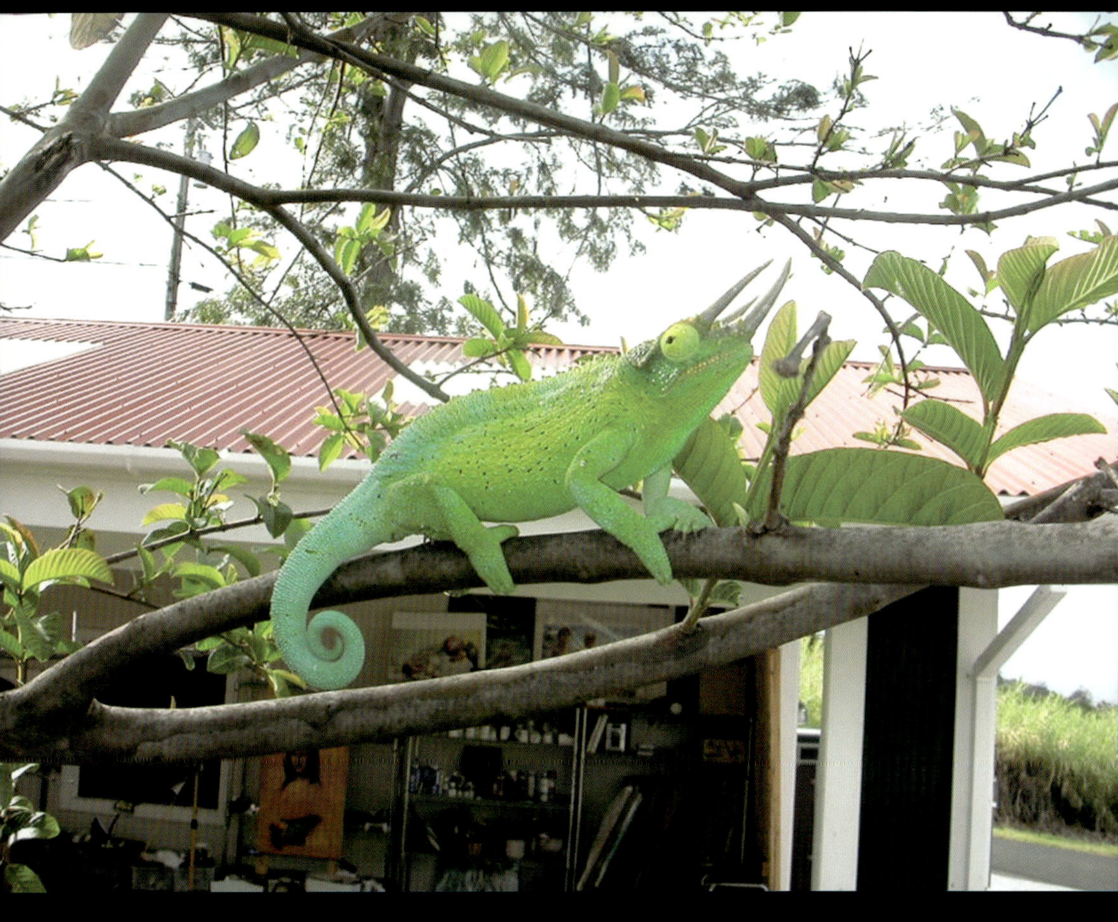

This photo, showing my studio in the background, was taken while the painting, "Why is this Woman Smiling" was in progress. Spunk Bob owned this guava tree and was easy to spot because of the bright suit he wore to impress the females that also resided in the tree. I like to think we are the ones in the enclosure as we view chameleons in their habitat, which just happens to be our garden.

Front Entrance with Areca Palms

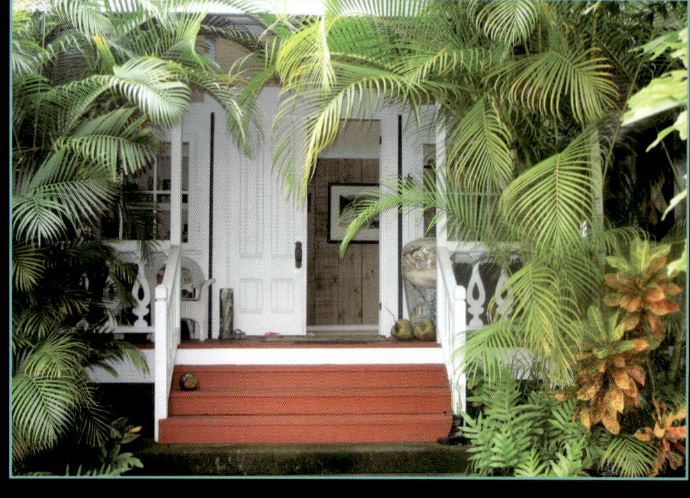

Chameleons can be found very close to human activity.

"Cham Country"

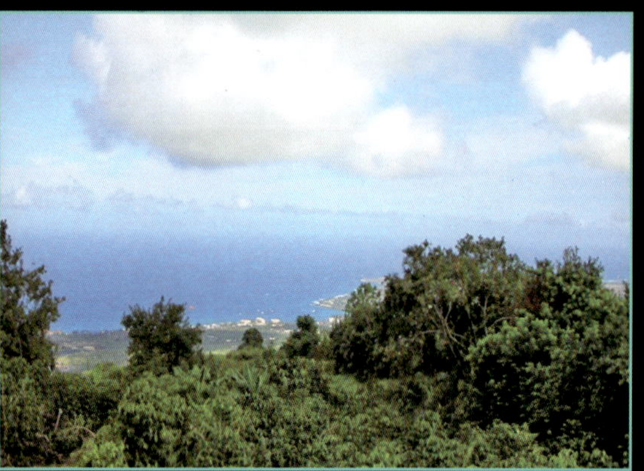

The chameleons on our property have come from the surrounding coffee farms and forested areas.

Gulp, that was a Good Fly

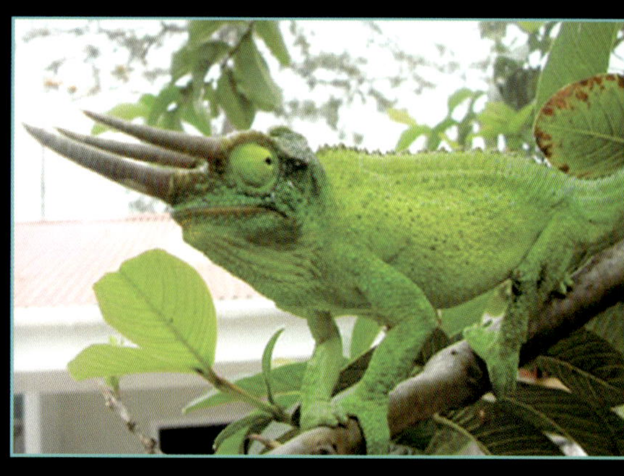

King Longhorns

I Used to Interact with Them

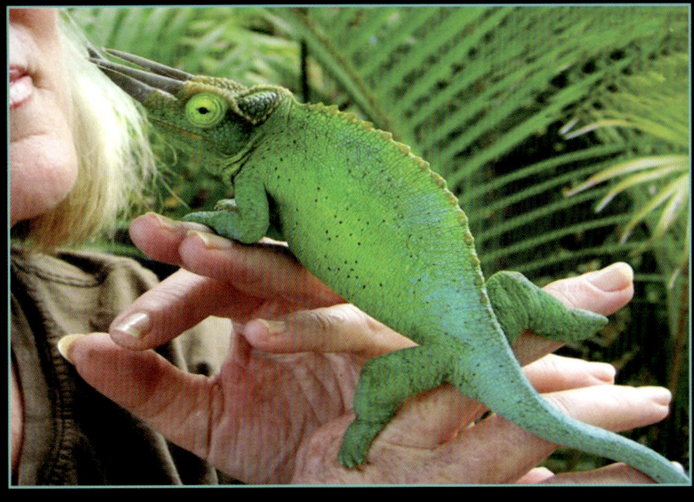

Now, I am more interested in watching their natural behavior, without disturbing them.

At the Watering Hole

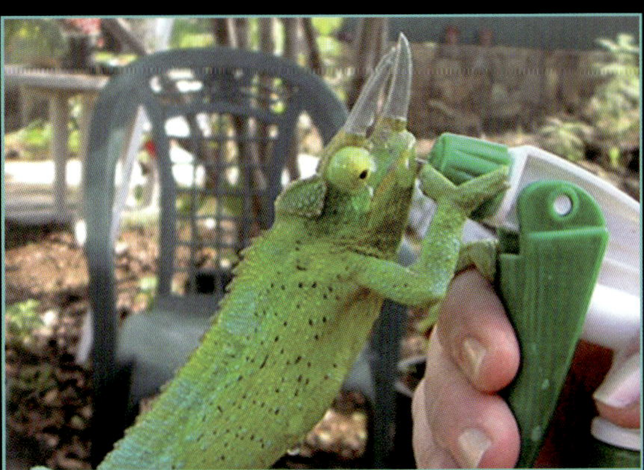

They are free to come and go. Many have become longtime residents. We have named some of the individuals and see them as living art.

Spunky on my Foot

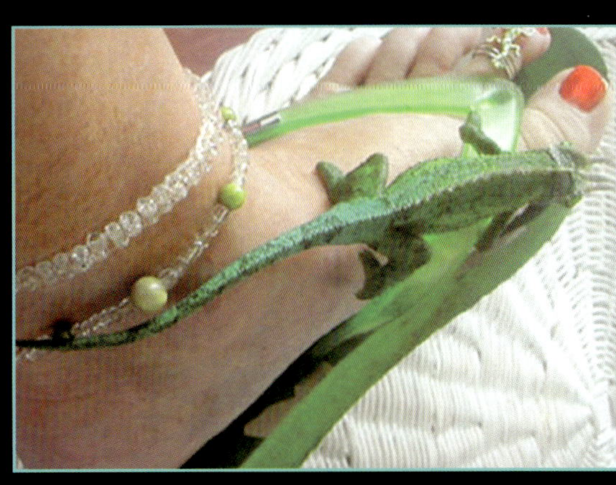

Photos on this page by Matt Lovein

Scout and Tina

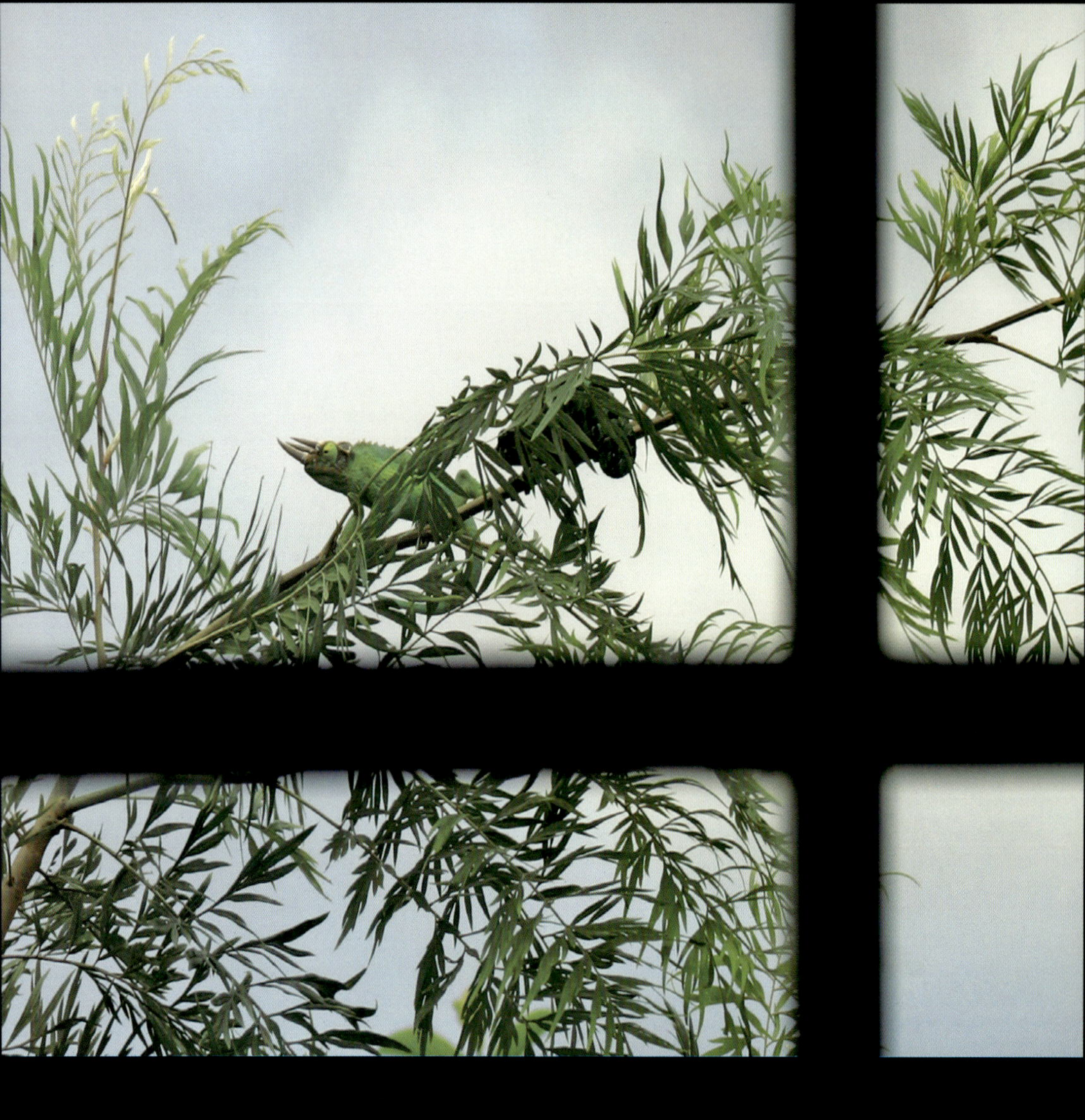

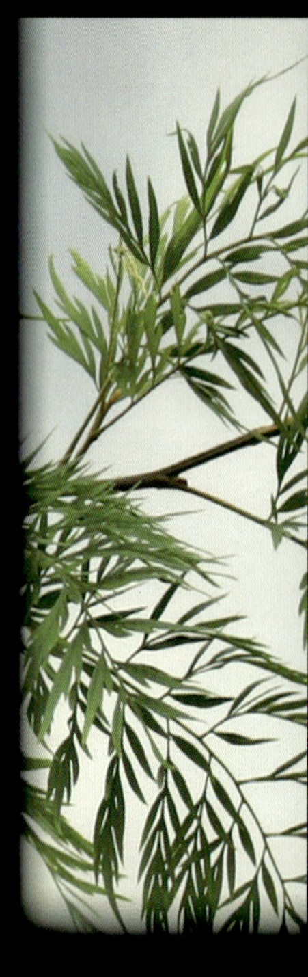

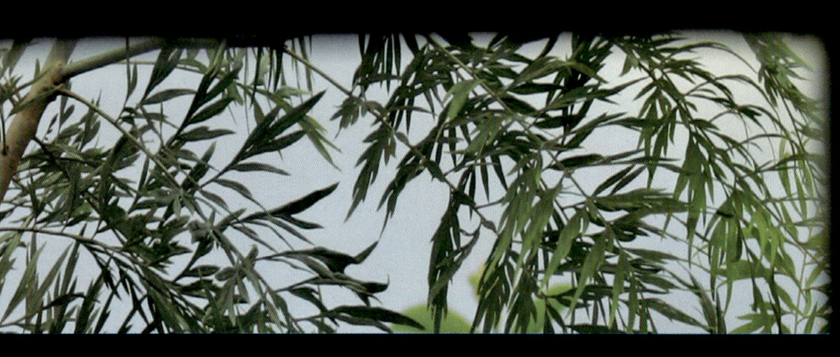

Looking Out

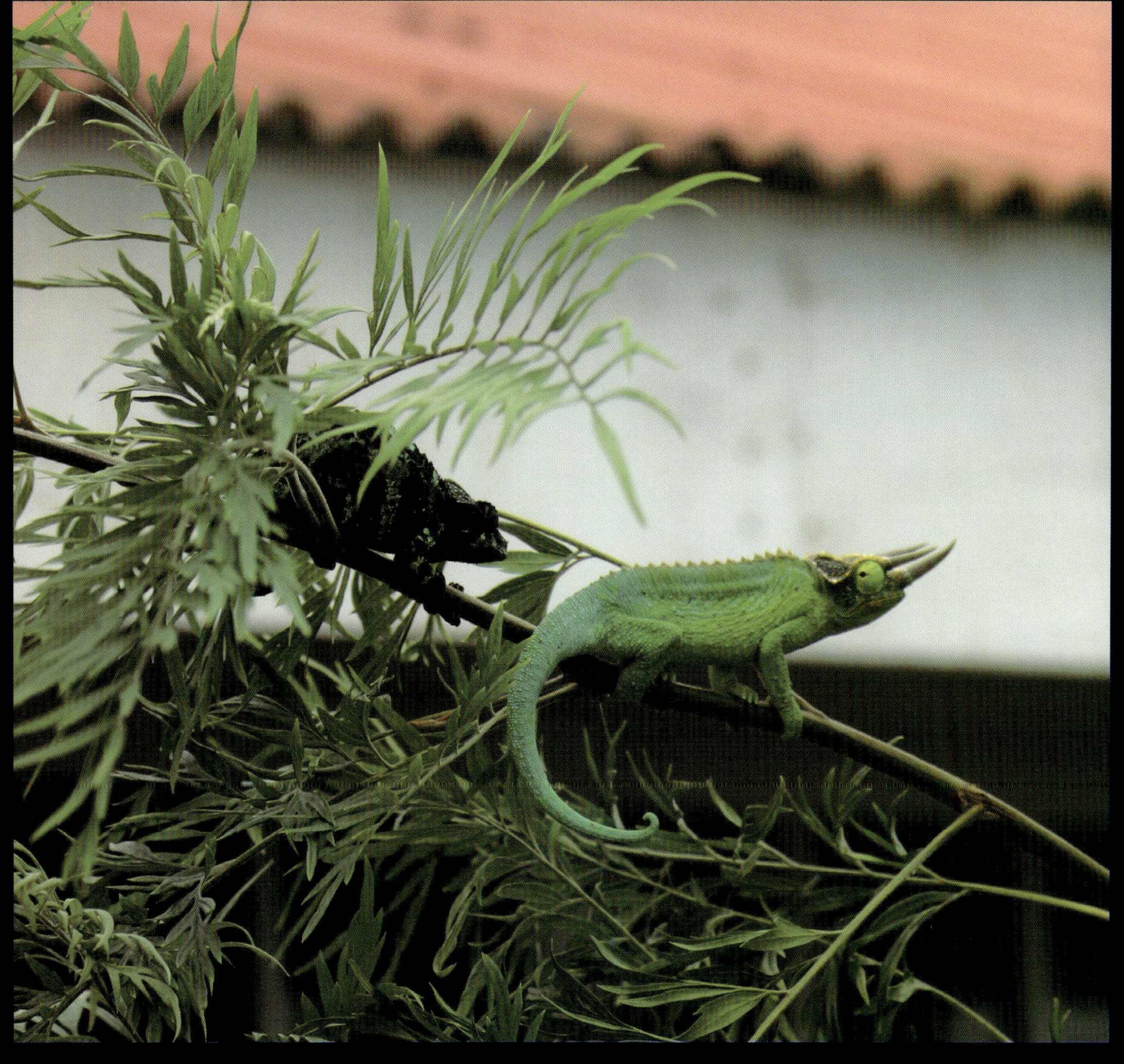

Looking In

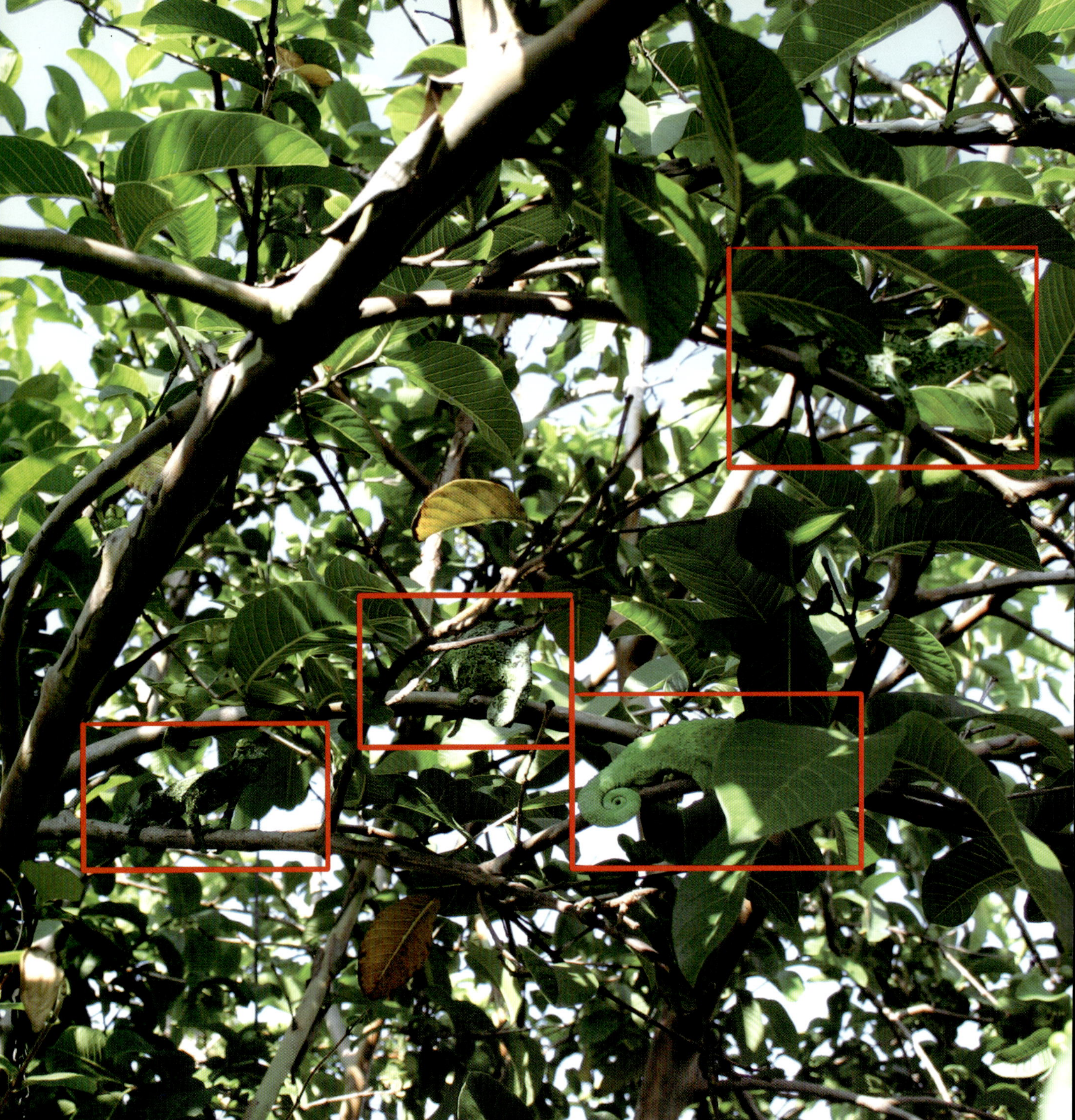

Look for What is Not the Tree

Even when chameleons are in plain sight, they are easily missed. It takes practice to see them. It is tricky because plants have similar colors, shapes and textures. Many times when I look at trees and bushes, I see what I think is a chameleon and it turns out to be a leaf or some other organic plant matter, or it can be just the other way around.

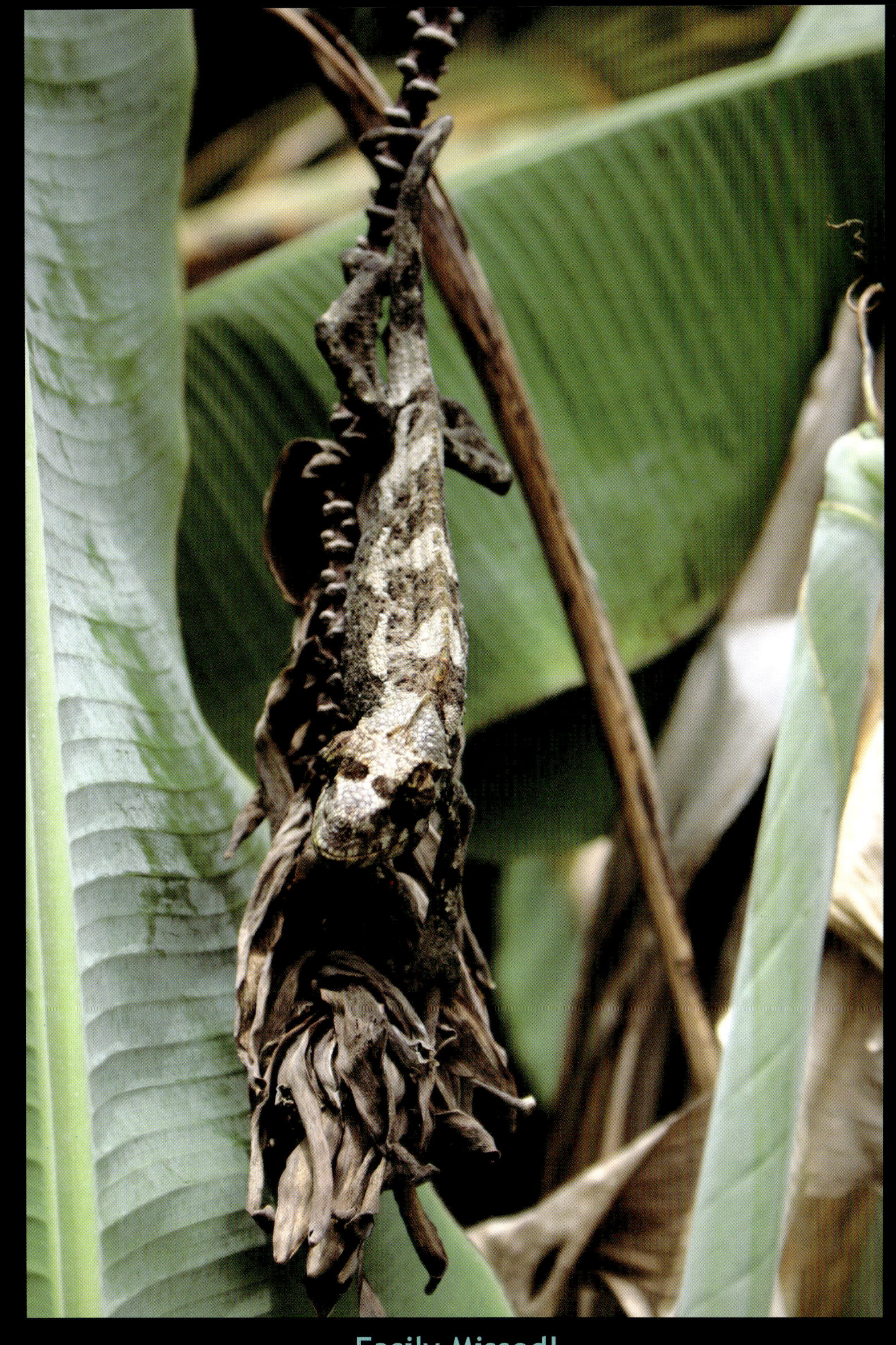

Easily Missed!

While folklore tells us chameleons control their appearance to blend with their surroundings, it is more likely their colors and patterns bear an uncanny resemblance to elements of their habitat, resulting in protective camouflage.

Sisty Specklers

Adult females can often be found in close proximity to each other. This is not true of adult males, which are more territorial.

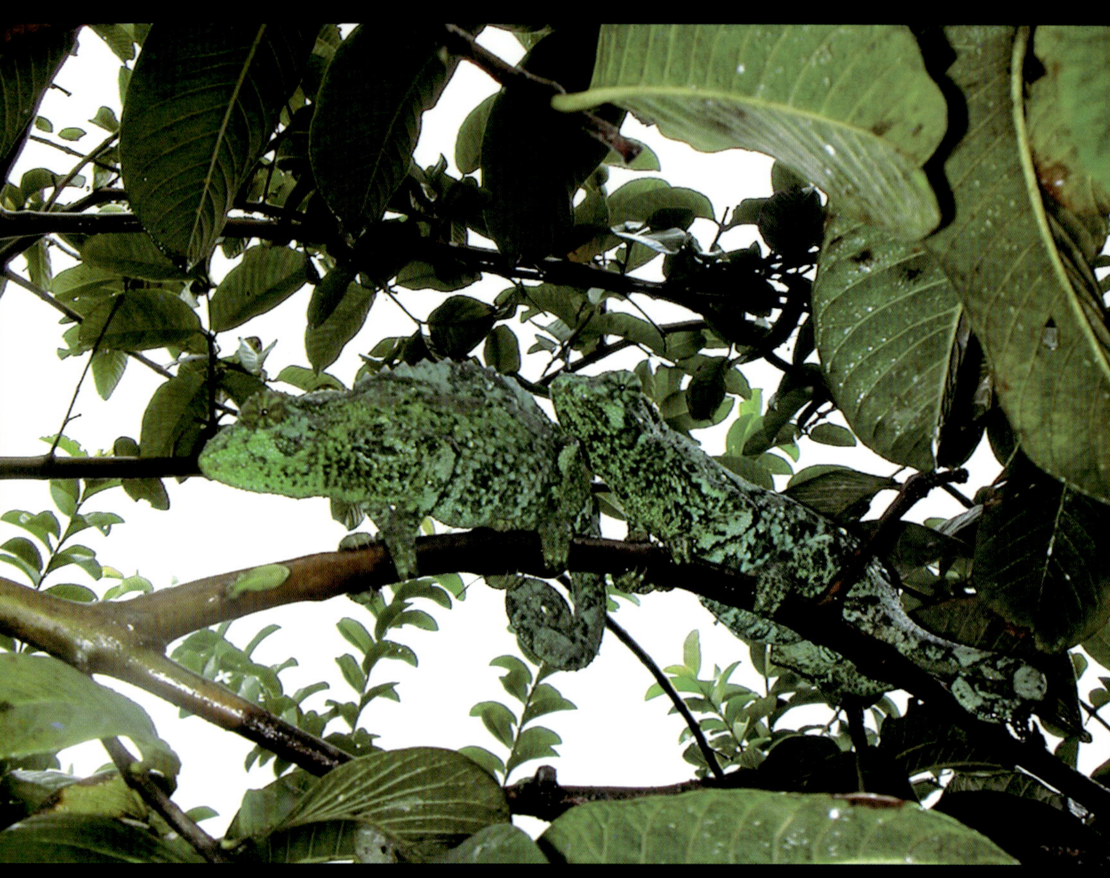

Unreceptive females develop patterns or speckles when a male displays breeding signals, such as head bobbing. These two were nearly solid green until a male approached. One of the ways females communicate their status is through their appearance. Additional factors that may affect skin changes include age, health, stress level, body temperature and threats from predators. Compared to males, female color variations are more pronounced and occur more frequently. They usually remain drab until fully mature and then they may become as vibrantly colored as males.

Guava Gals

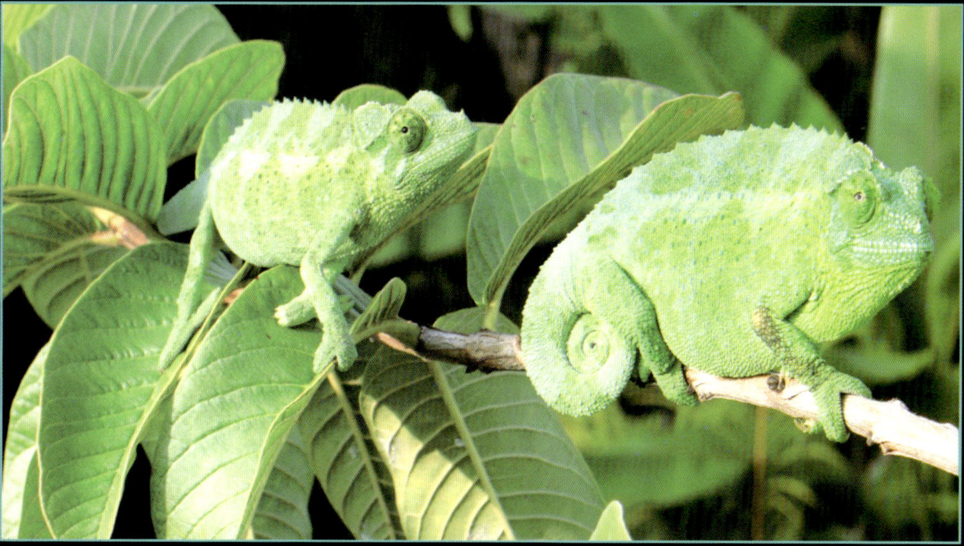

It appears from their resting colors, there is no male in sight.

Blenda

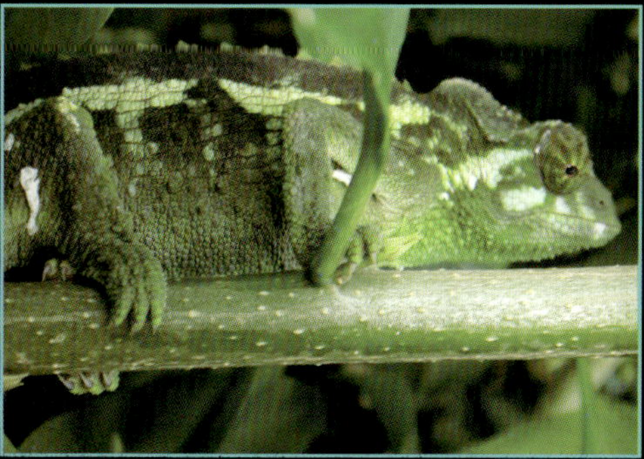

In the Night Blooming Jasmine

Spirilina

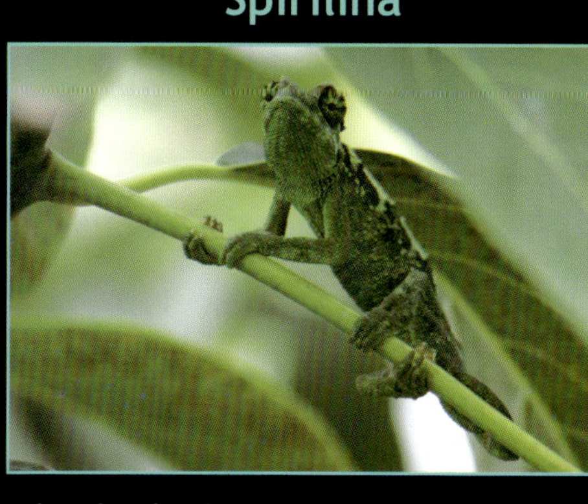

This little female is exceptionally green for her young age.

Dominant Female

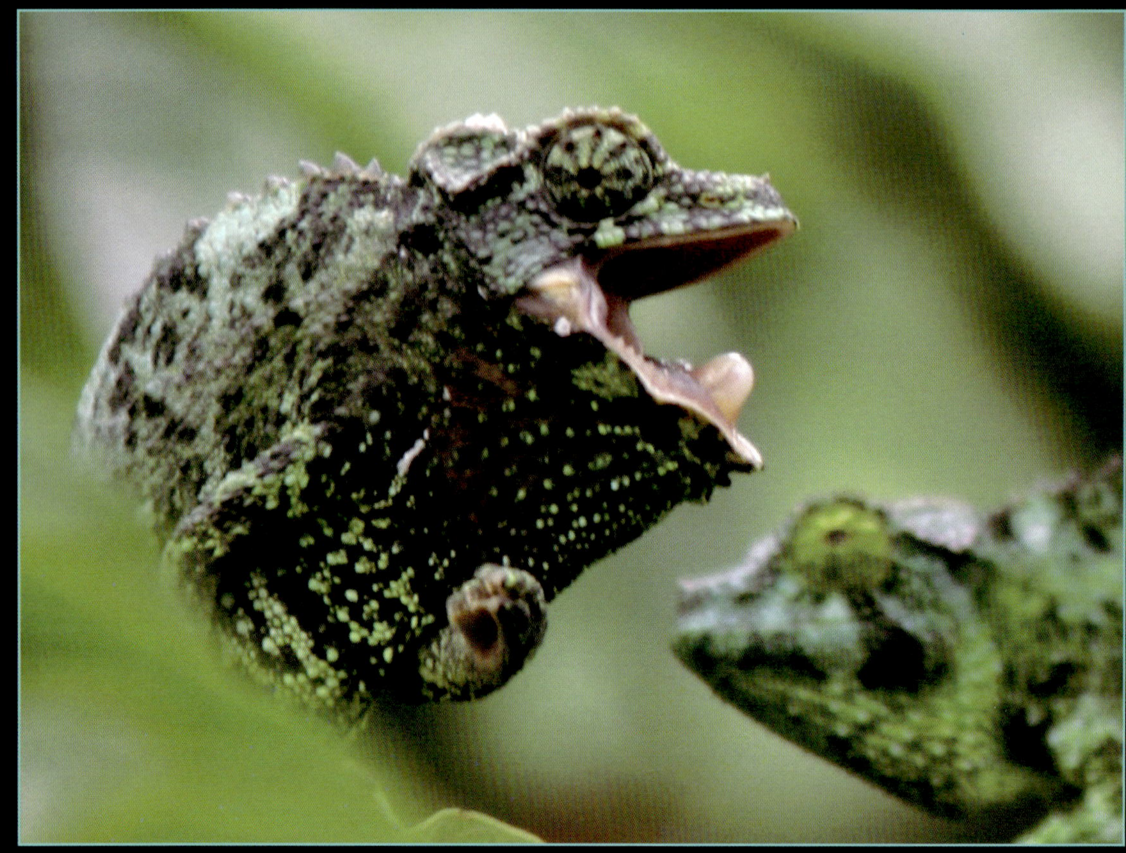

These two females had to sort things out before sharing the same tree.

Settling Down for the Night

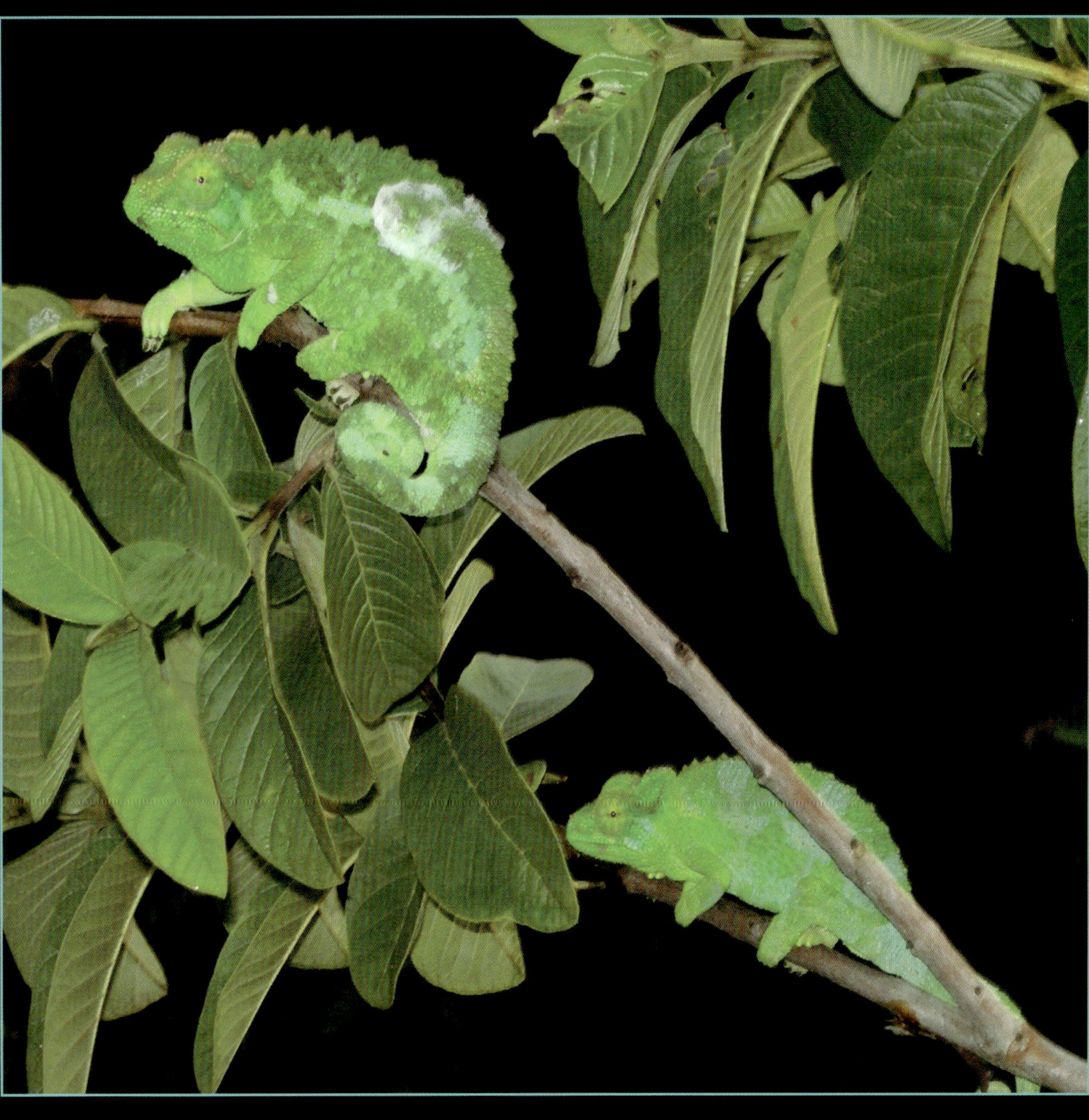

After collecting the last rays of the sun and as darkness approaches, they find a preferred branch where they feel safe. Because chameleons are diurnal animals, they are active with eyes open throughout the daylight hours, though they may perch in the same spot for hours, even days.

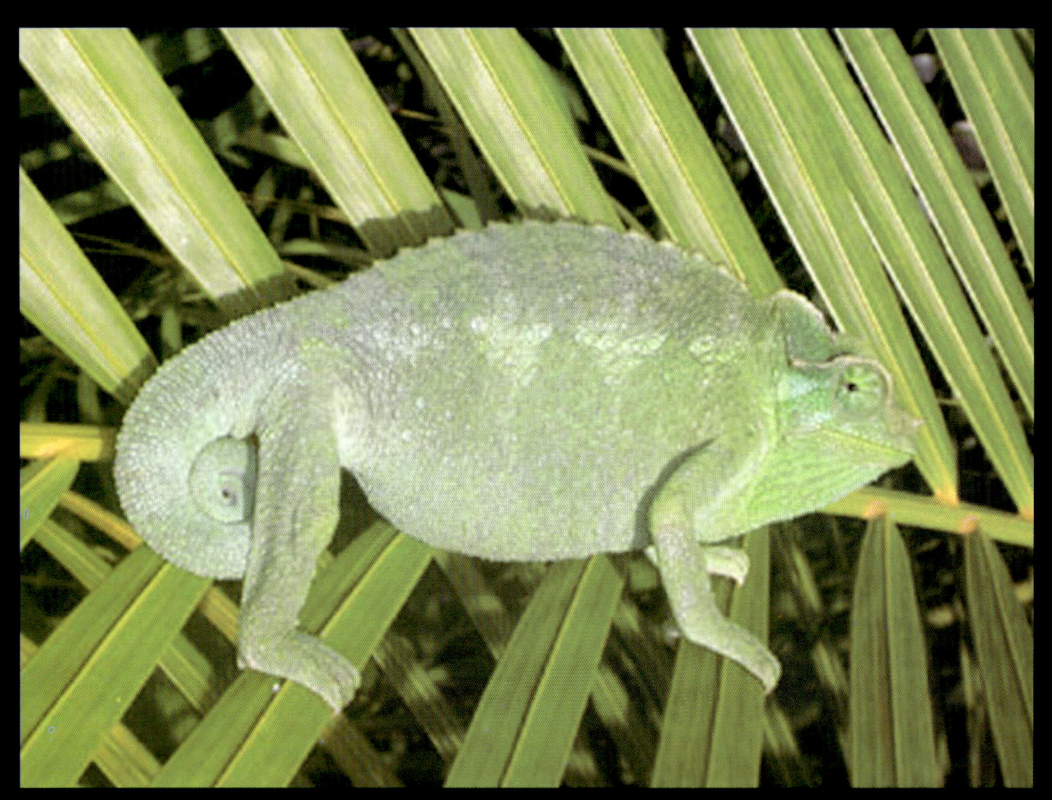

Basking

This female is flattening out like a solar panel to make the most of the morning sun. A chameleon can also turn dark to absorb more heat, which is a better option for a female that is full with babies. Since they are cold blooded animals, they need to warm up after a nighttime drop in temperature.

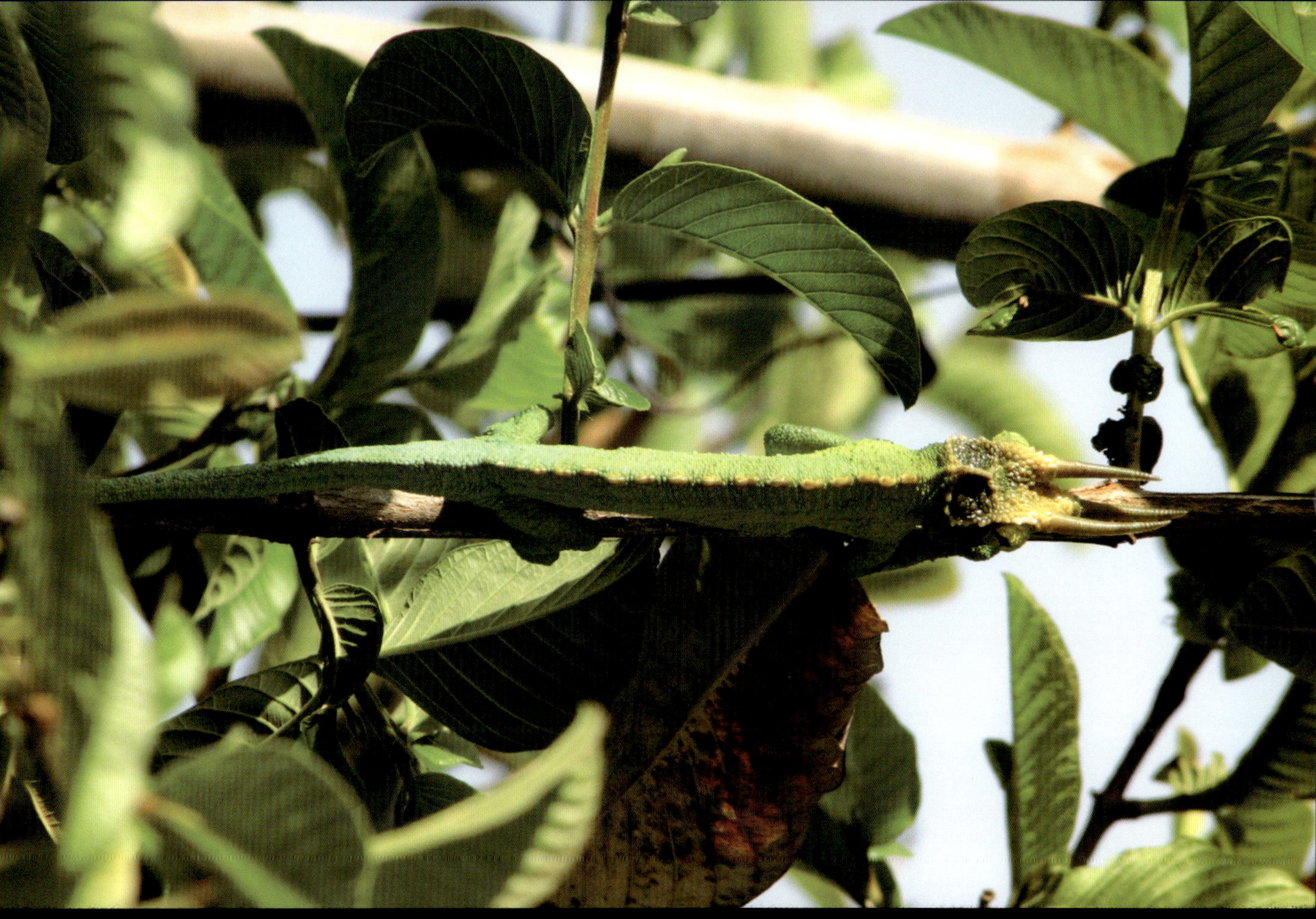

Shadowing

This is an example of a chameleon making himself almost as thin as the branch. His shape, combined with the color of the foliage surrounding him, provides an effective camouflage and from the opposite side, he is hardly visible. Longtime residents are familiar with Matt and me, and have learned we are not predators, so they rarely hide when they see us. When someone new comes into their realm, they often shadow in the tree.

Breathe the Morning

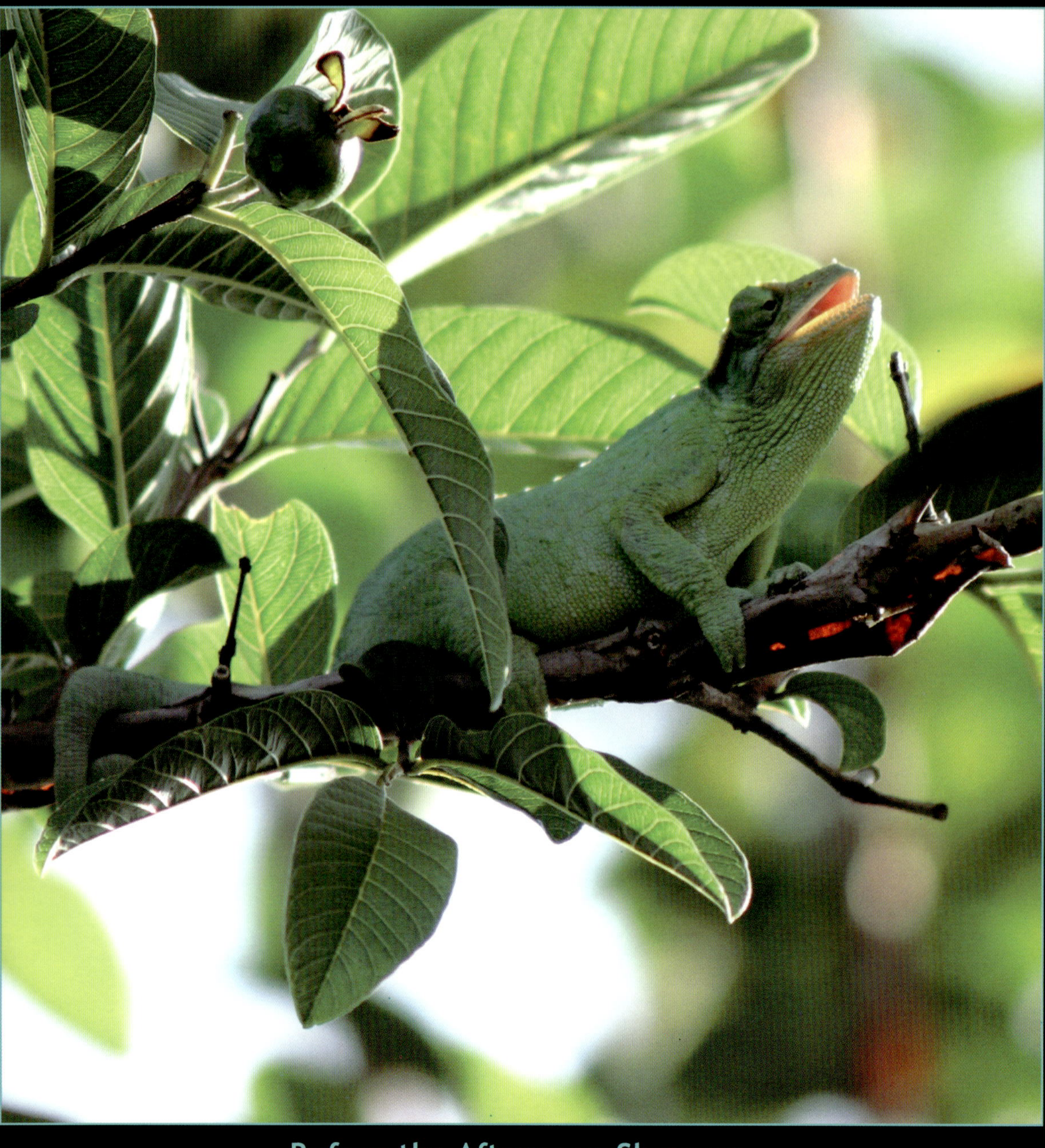

Before the Afternoon Showers

Salute to the Sun

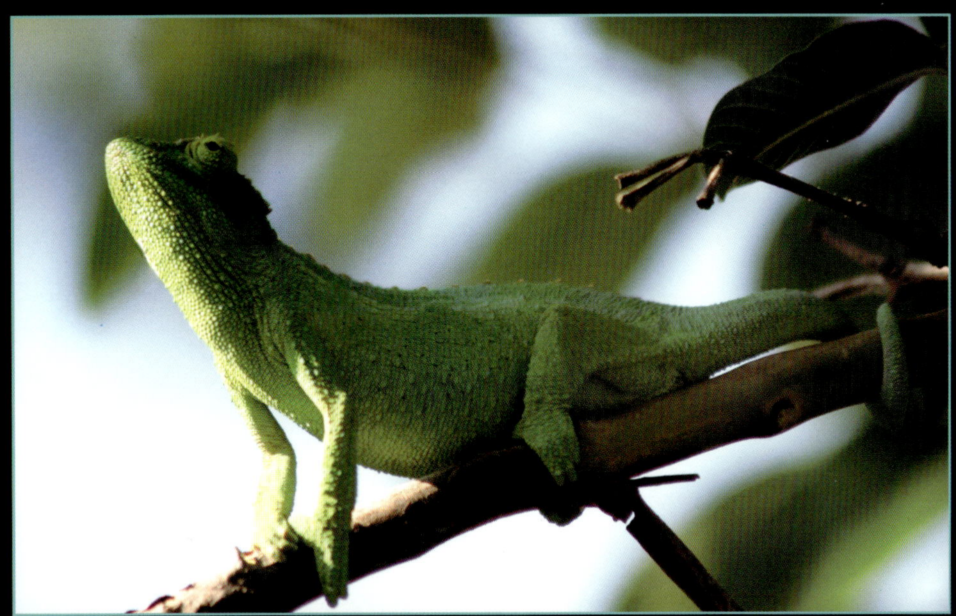

Gravid (pregnant)

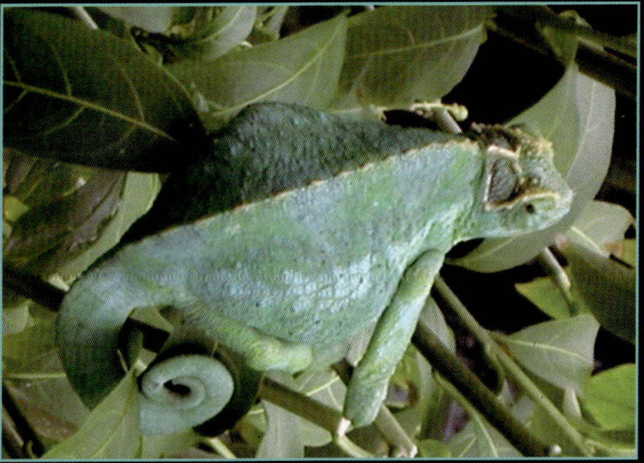

Gestation is approximately seven months. It may be shorter or longer, depending on temperature and possibly rainfall, which also affects food availability. The cycle continues throughout the entire life of the animal. Births usually occur on a warm and sunny day, with the delivery of anywhere between one and forty live neonates. The number depends on a combination of factors, such as age and size of the female.

Gaping and Showing Stress Pattern

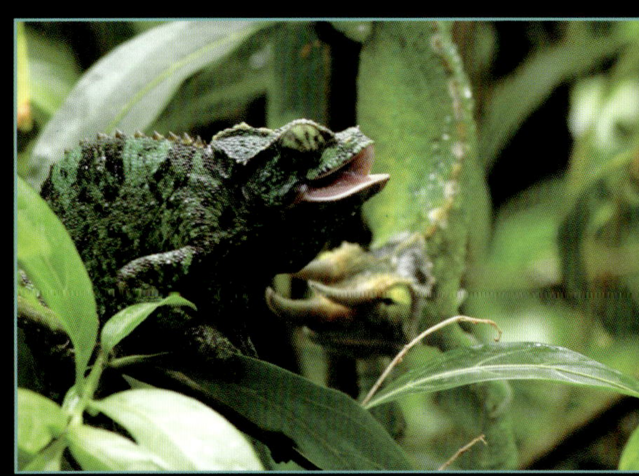

This female is communicating to the male that she is not receptive to his advances. She changes her body shape to appear as menacing as possible and she gapes, in what I refer to as the "silent scream." If the male continues to pursue against her wishes, she can become dark or even black. She also displays non-receptivity by rocking from side to side, swaying like a leaf or a dead twig blowing in the wind.

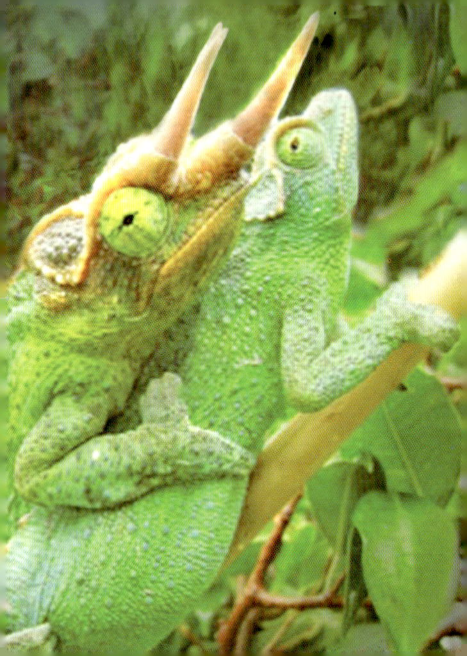

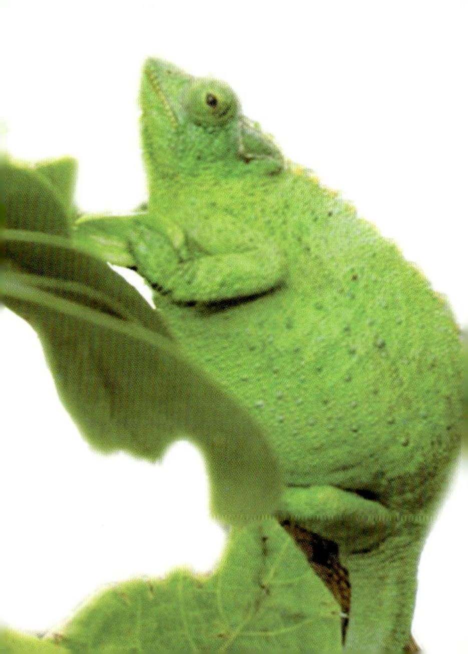

Newborns

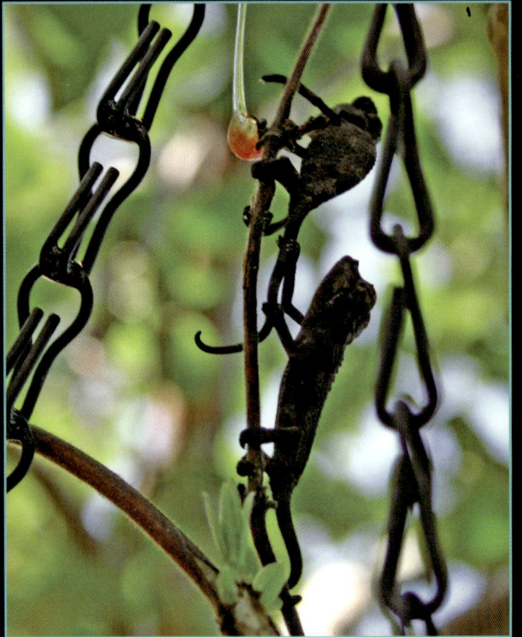

Almost immediately, they have the ability to climb.

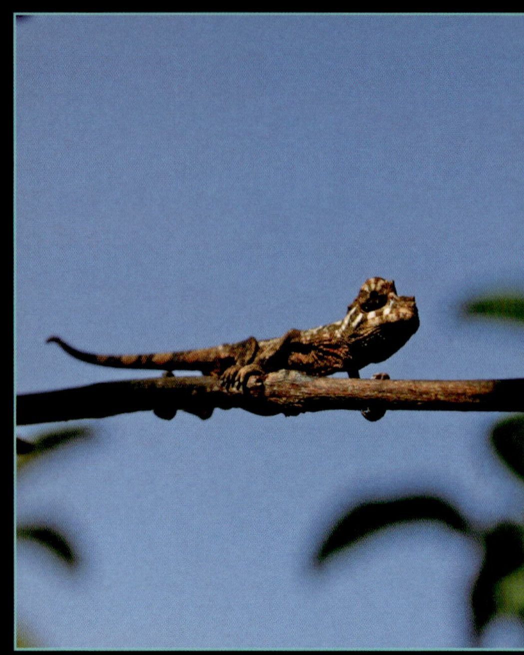

They display many of the same movements and features as adults.

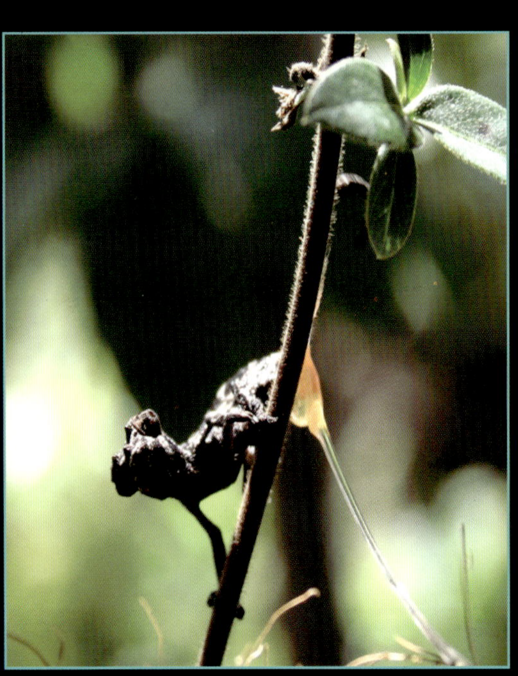

They are about one inch long.

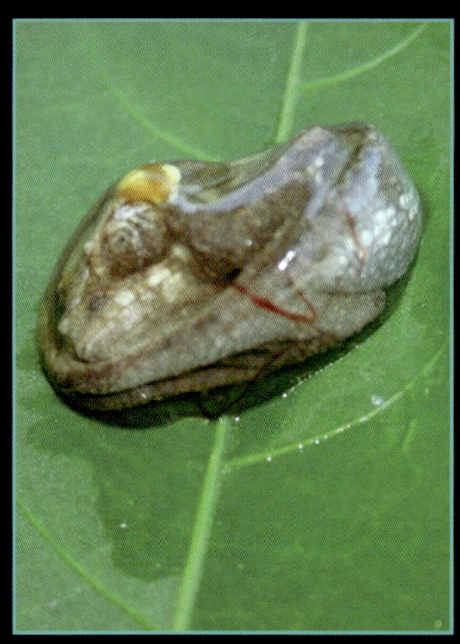

This is a neonate, getting its first view of the world from the embryonic sack.

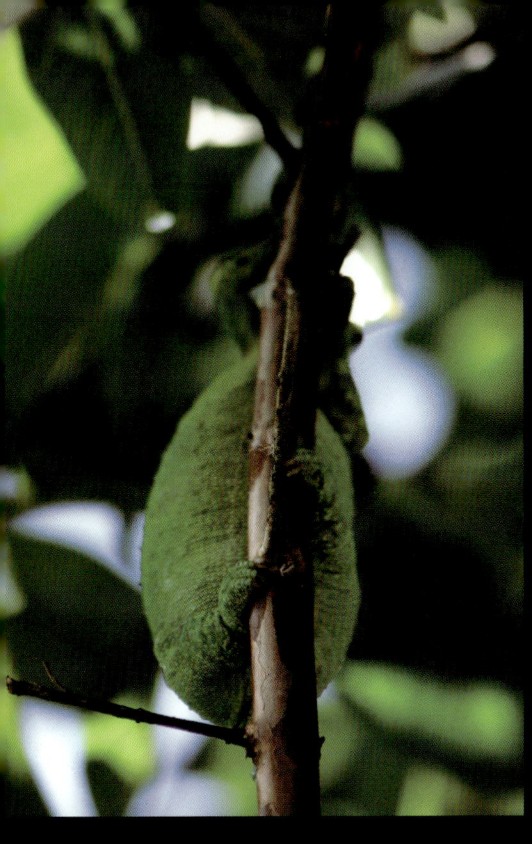

Births in the Guava Tree

Lulu decided to have babies in the hanging plant basket. She had ten or more live births and several unfertilized eggs that looked like little yolks.

As the neonates emerged, one at a time, their large eyes could be seen through the membrane that held them. Completely still at first, they soon fought to get out of the clear sack. Some of them were climbing around in the tree and some were in the basket. The mother chameleon does not feed or nurture the young. They are on their own from the minute they are born.

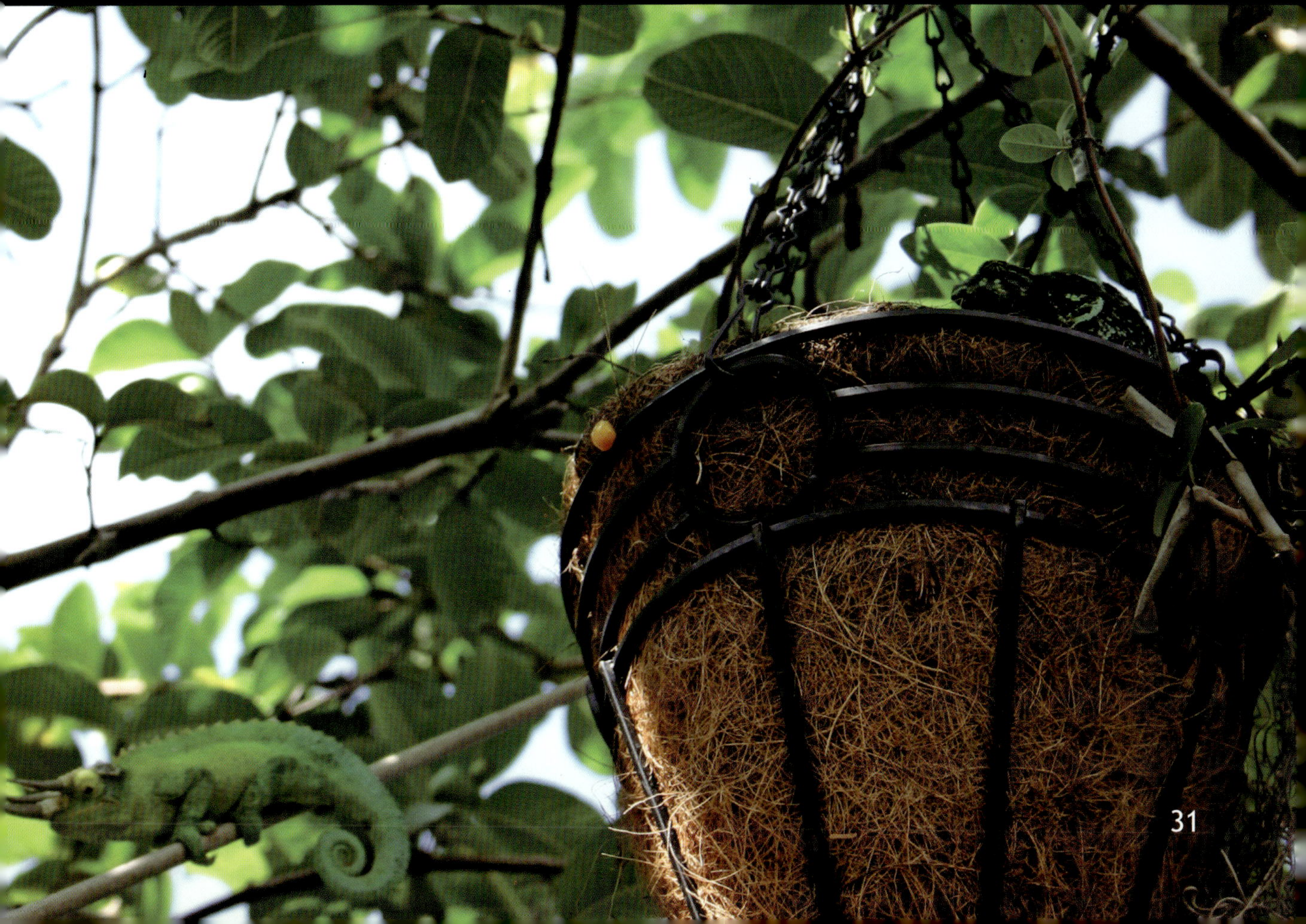

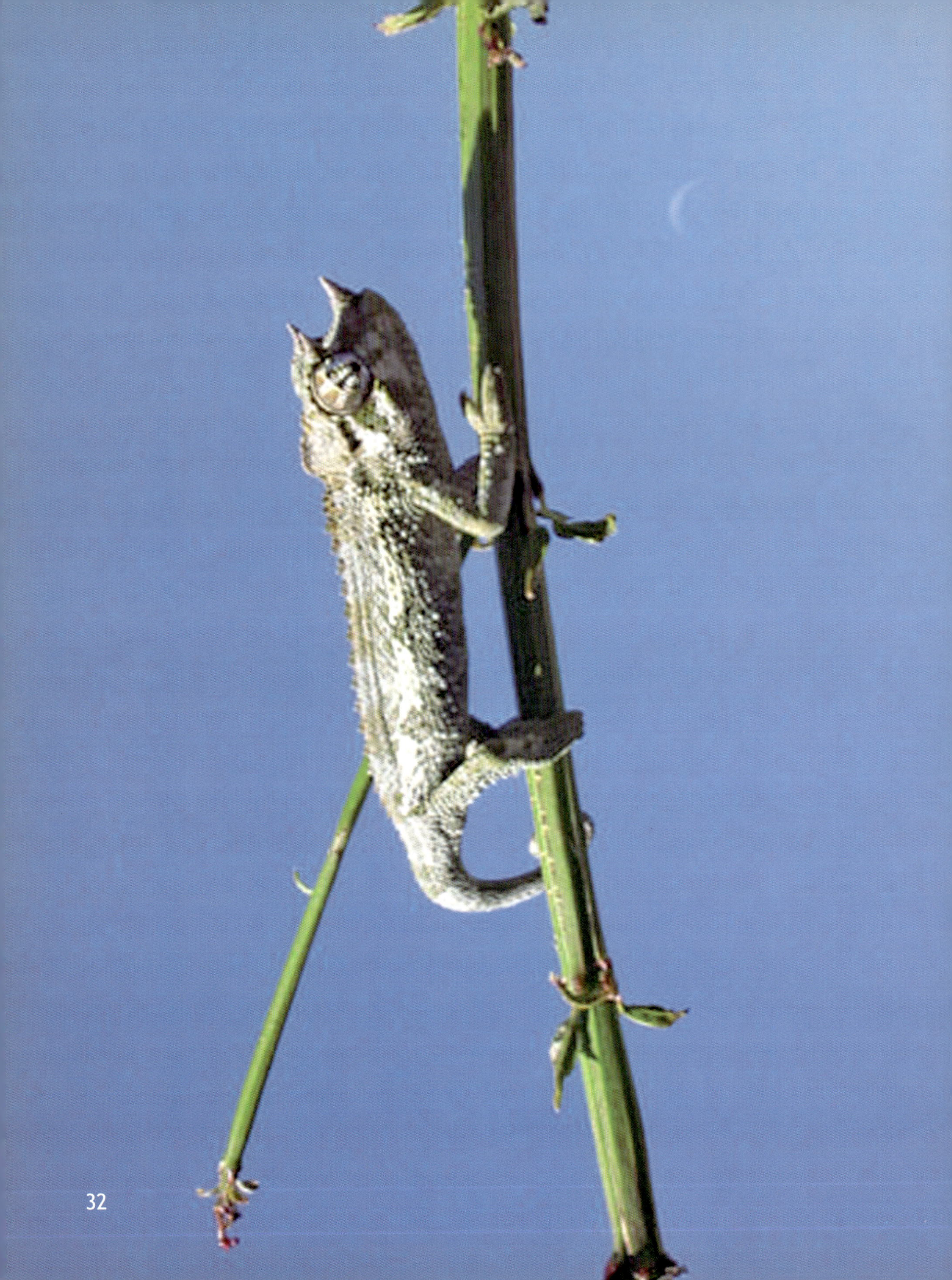

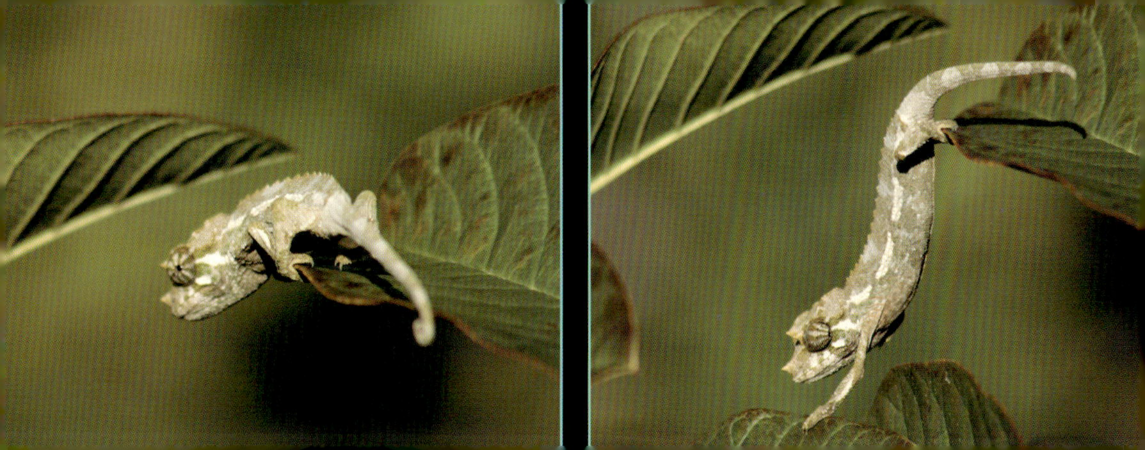

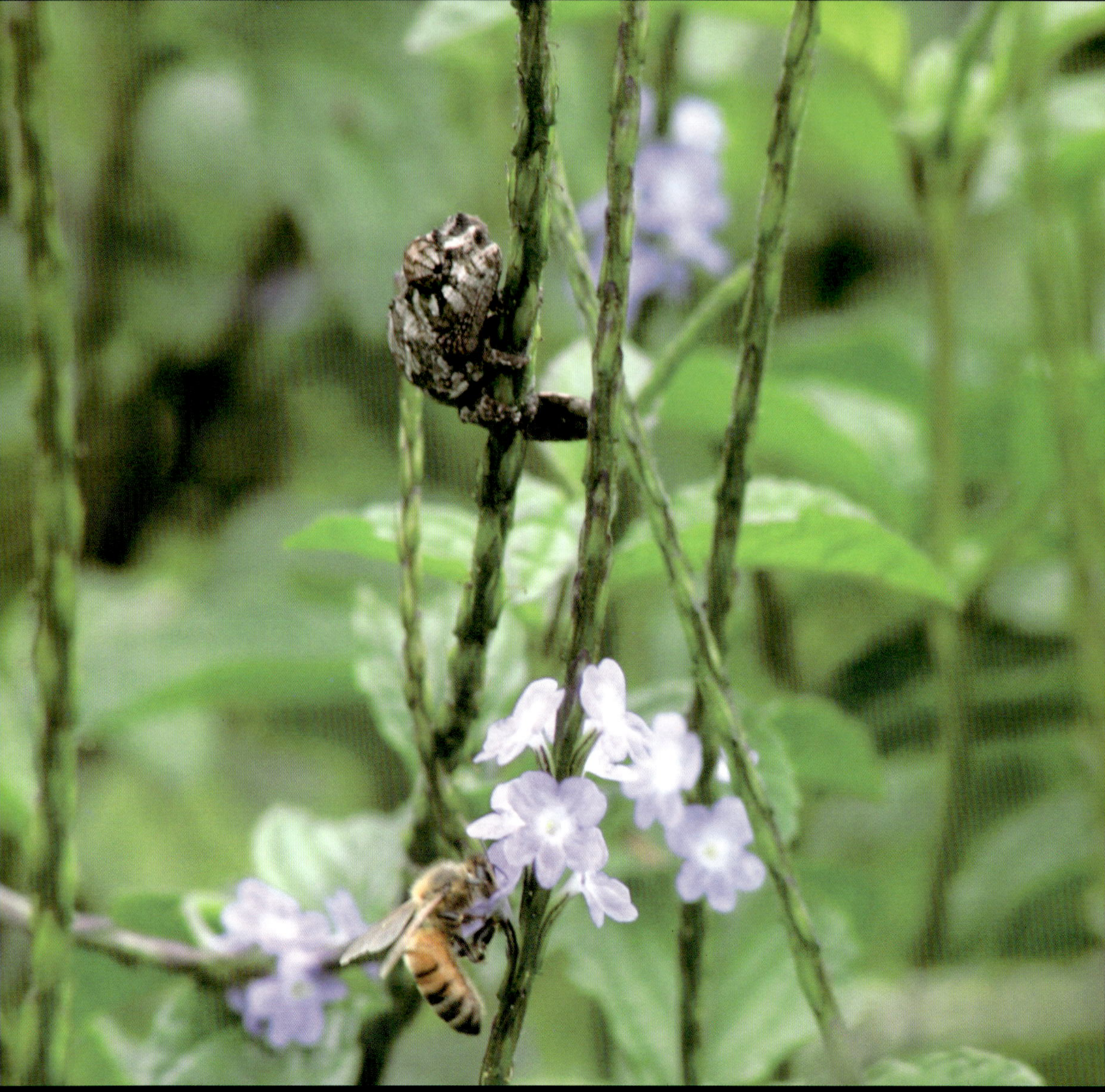

Babies usually are found in the lower foliage where the little stems and branches are just the right size for tiny feet. The bushes provide protection, filtered sunlight and shade. They hunt for small insects that have been attracted by blossoms or fallen fruit. The babies lick raindrops from leaves.

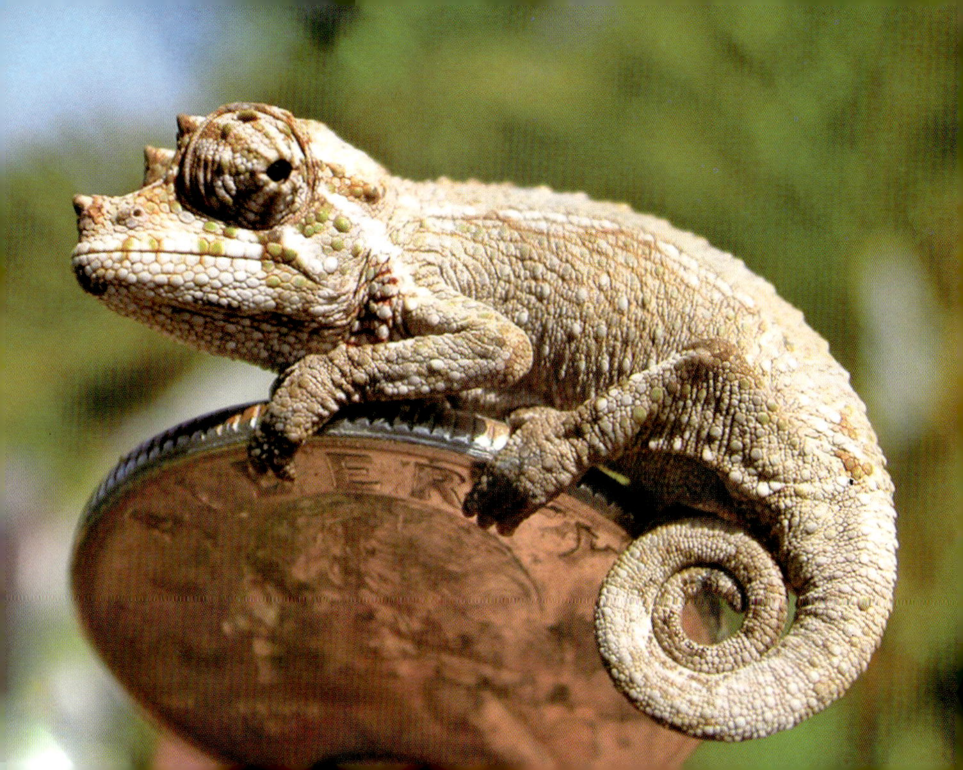

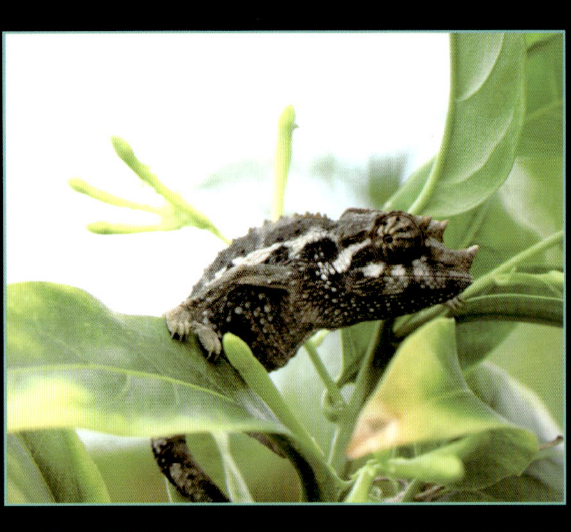

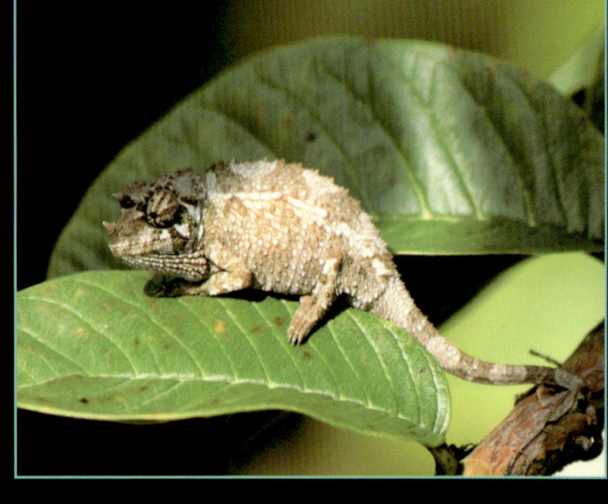

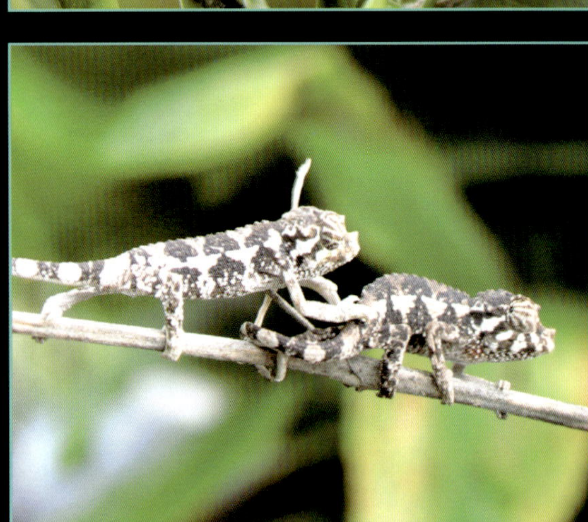

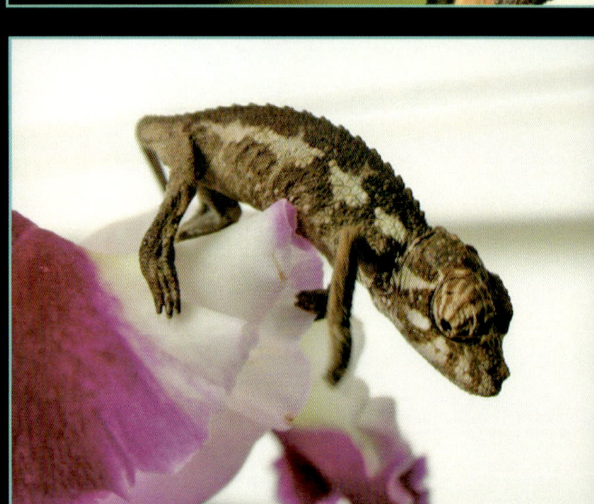

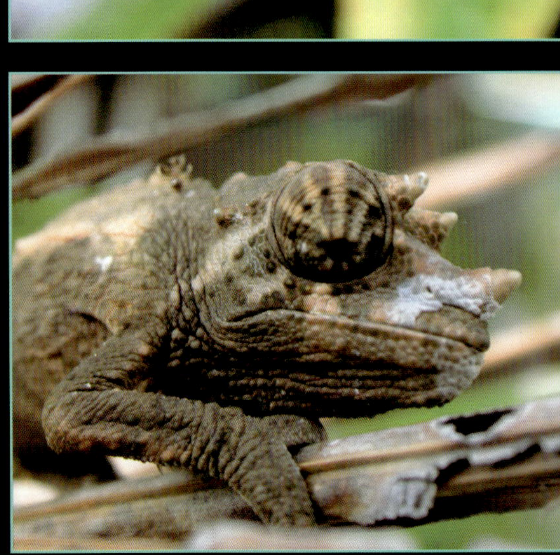

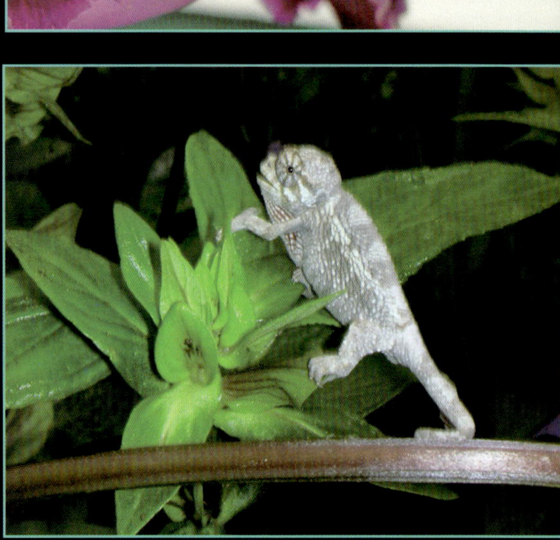

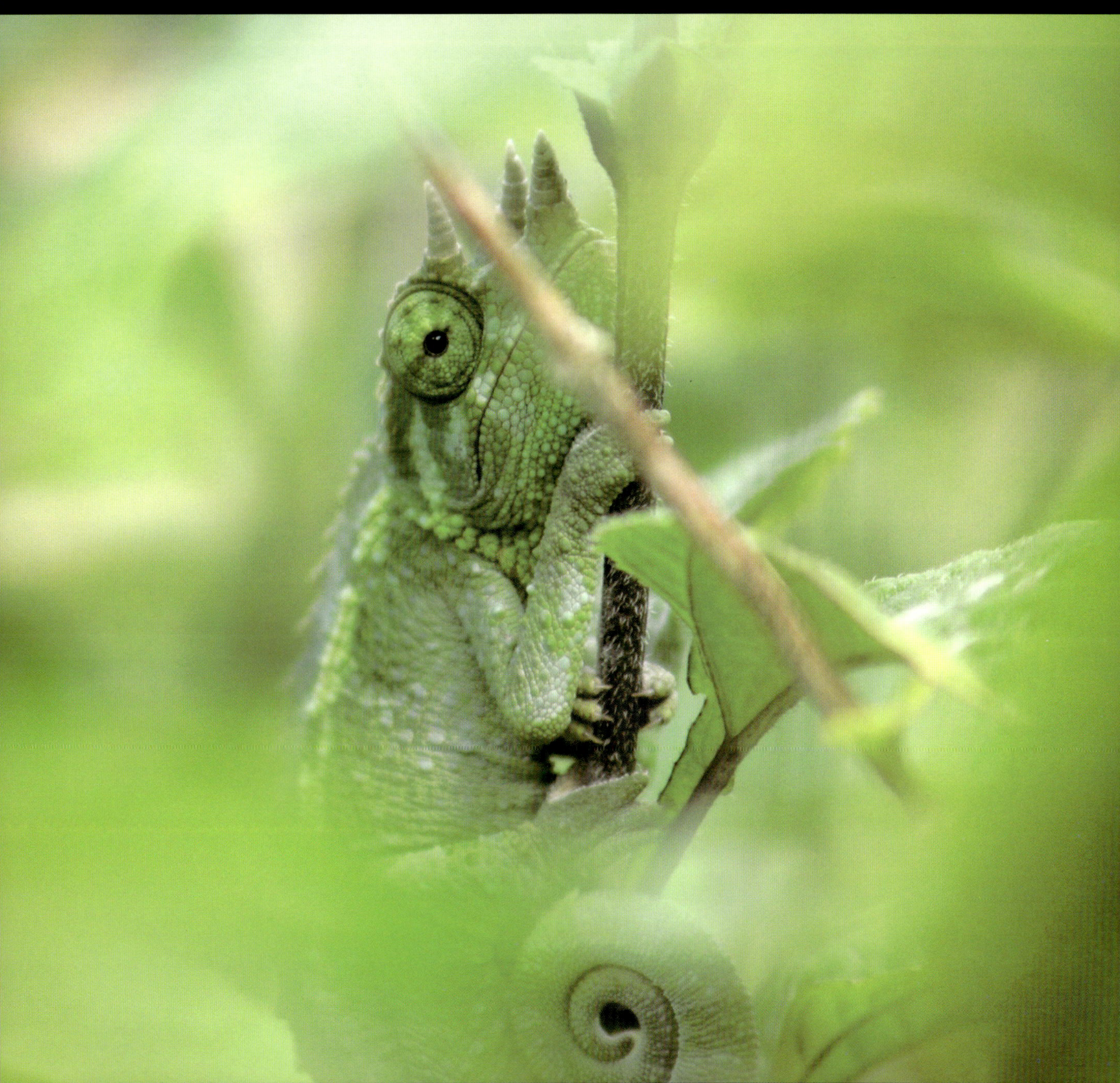

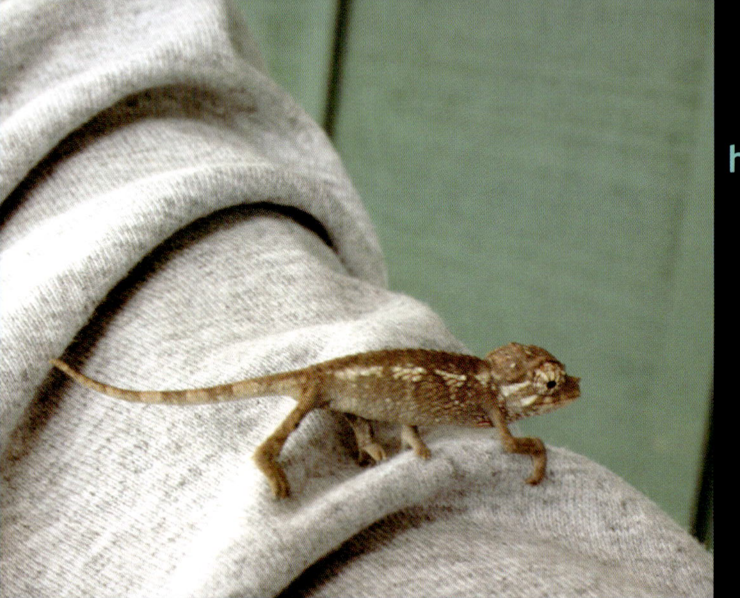

This little critter
had been climbing around
on Matt's shirt.

He must've hitchhiked
while Matt
was working
in the garden.

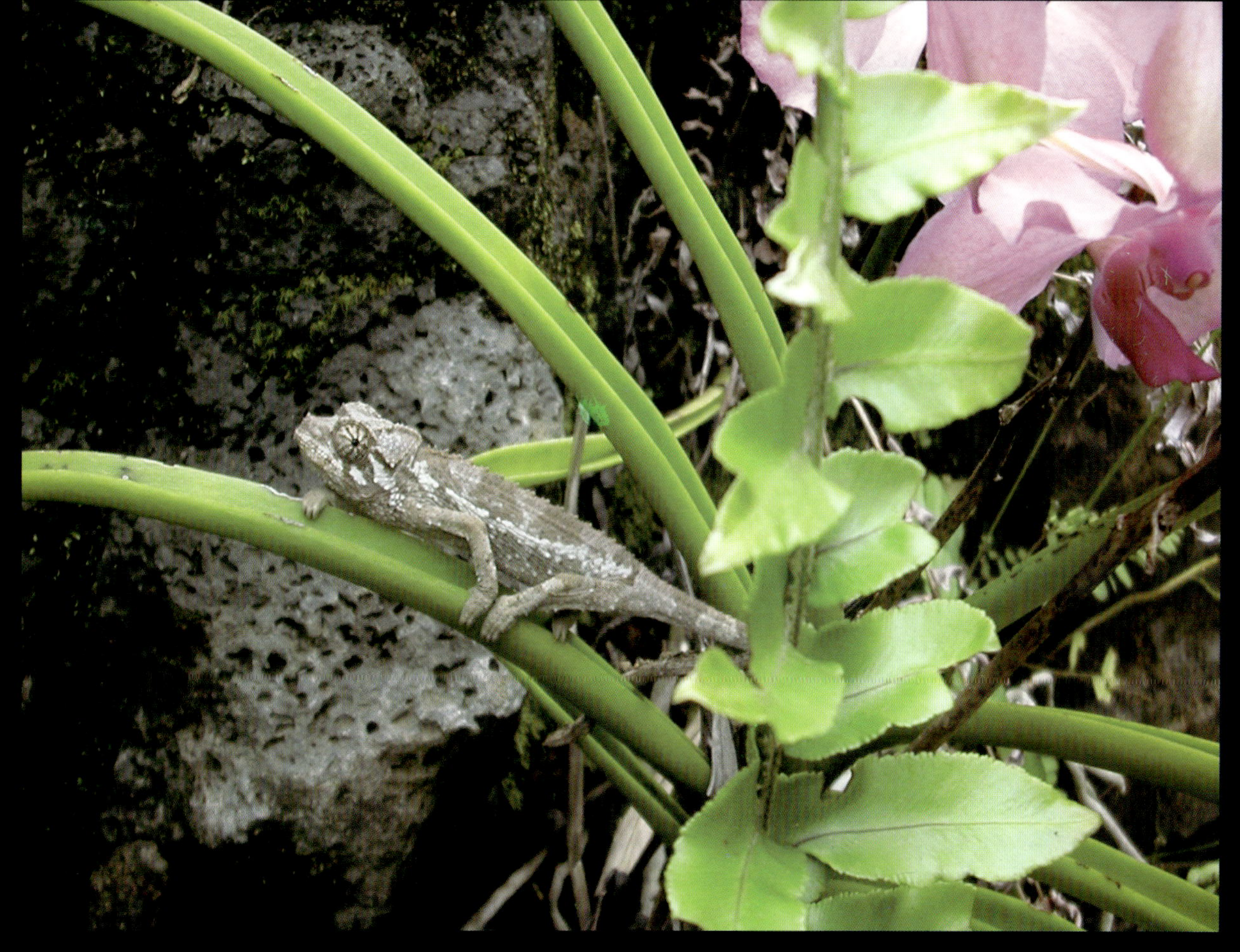

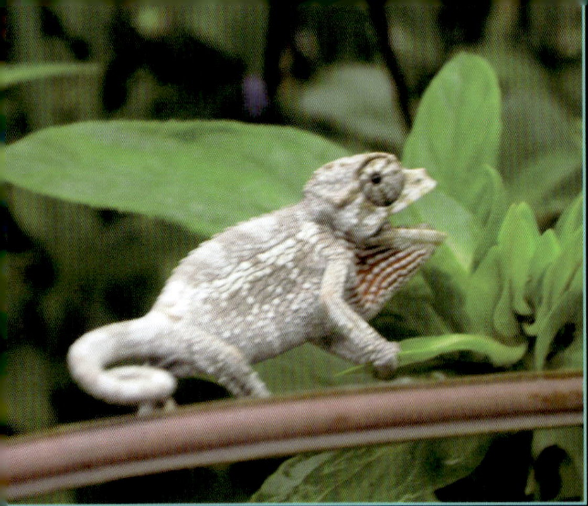

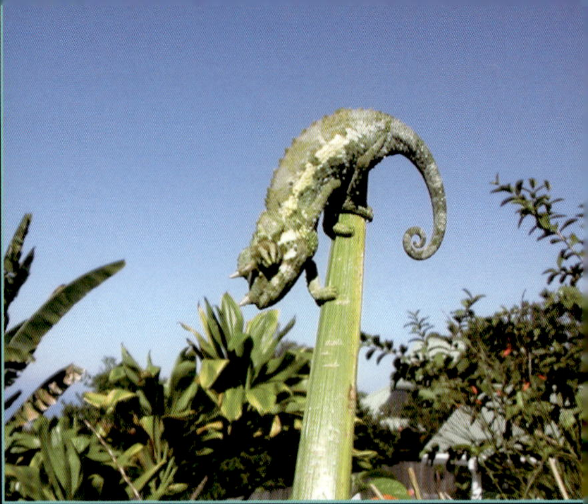

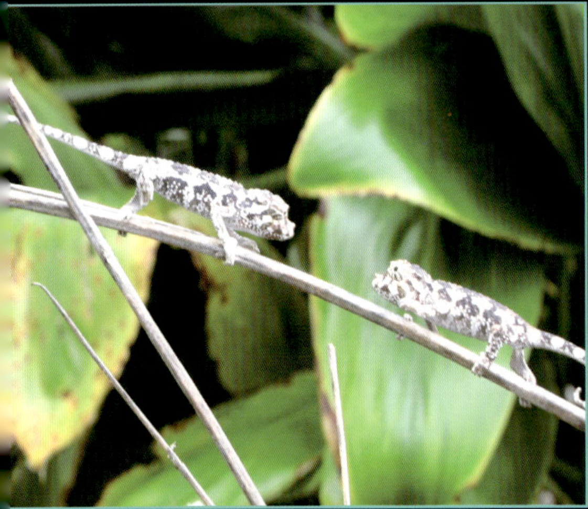

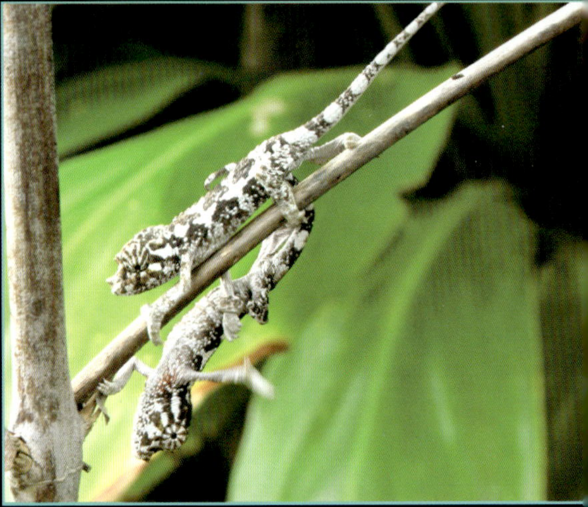

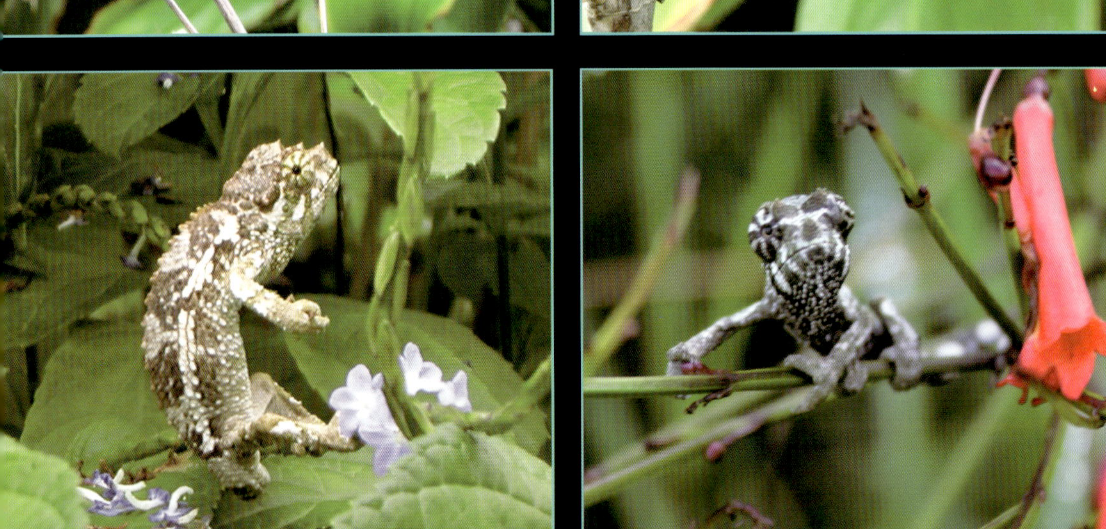

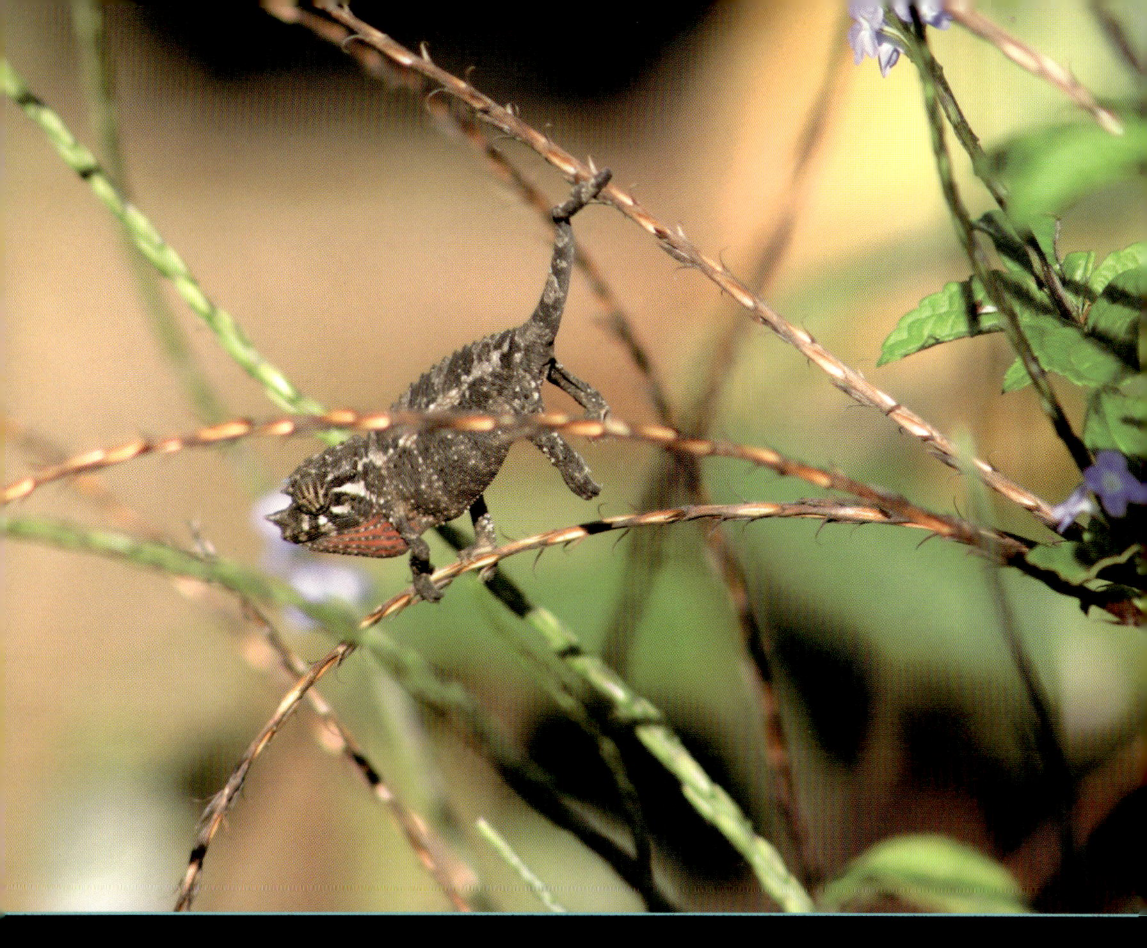

Red Gular

Red in the baby's gular (throat) indicates stress. Adults do not exhibit this color. Their patterns are reminiscent of paisley, hearts, diamonds or even a Navaho blanket and their colors range from charcoal and white to shades of brown, tan or beige. Staying close together for the first week or so, like a litter of kittens, they tumble and climb. Then they scatter and disappear deep inside the bushes. They are not easy to spot, wearing their little wild animal pajamas and blending with the mottled patterns of flickering sunlight, branches and leaves.

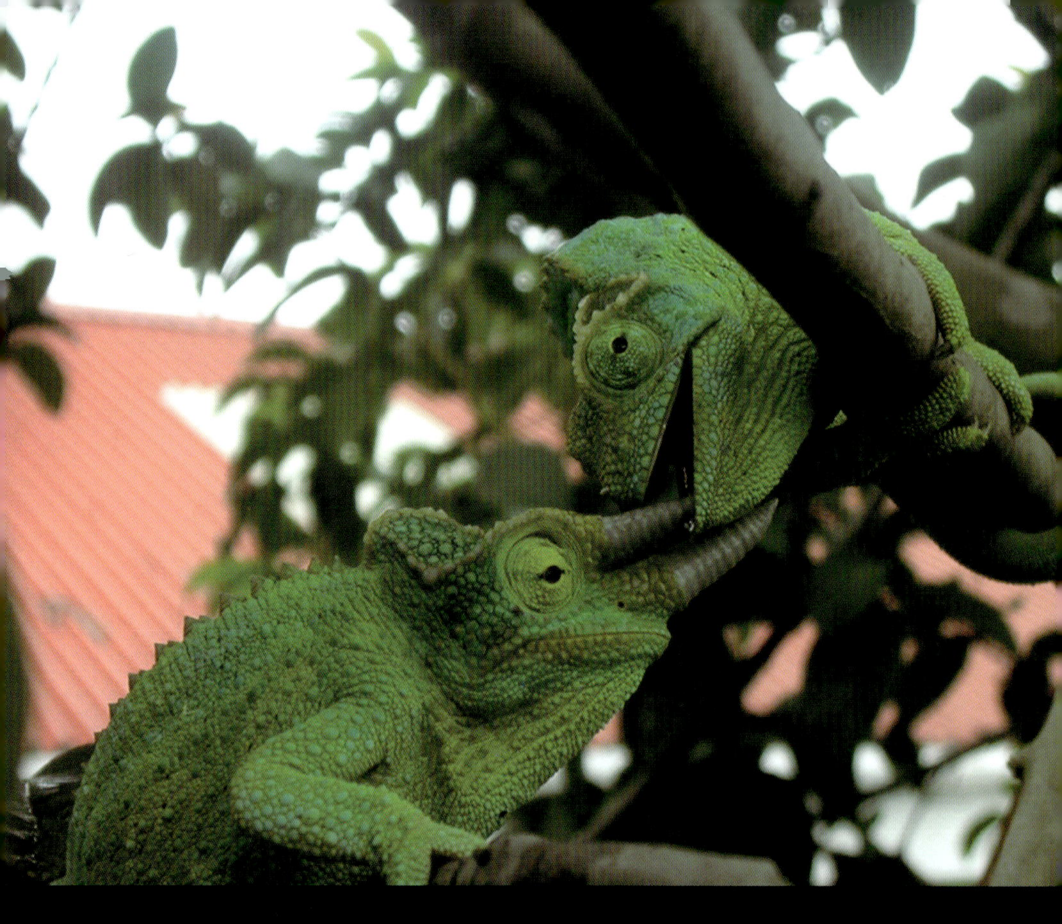

Love Bite

In this courtship, the female is biting the male's preocular horn. Often when the male and female interact, the female will grasp onto a horn, one of his feet or legs. The male uses his front feet like hands to caress or grab onto the female. Neither of these chameleons look to be stressed.

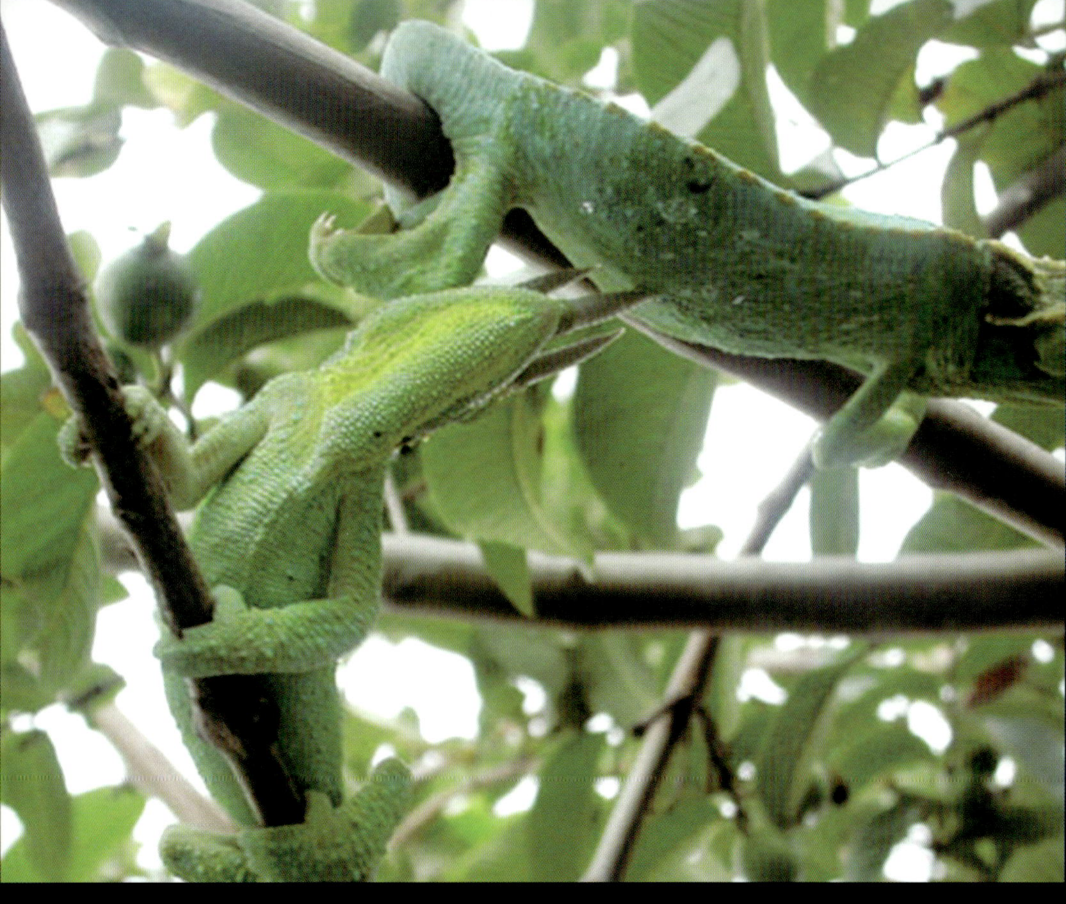

Courting

The male is using his horns to coax the female into position for mating. The window of opportunity, when the female is receptive, is very narrrow and he doesn't want to miss it.

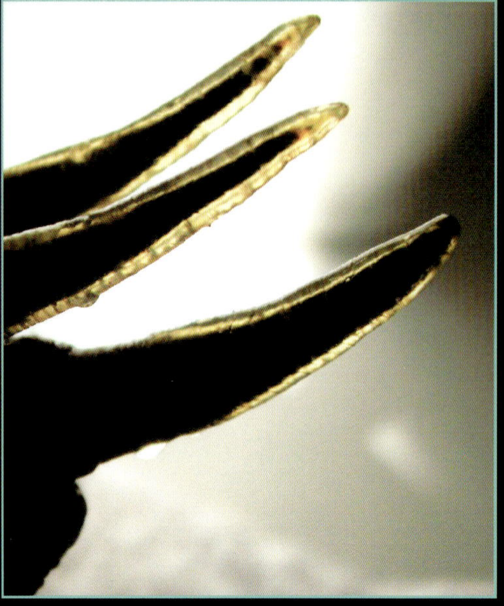

Jack

Horns have a keratin sheath.

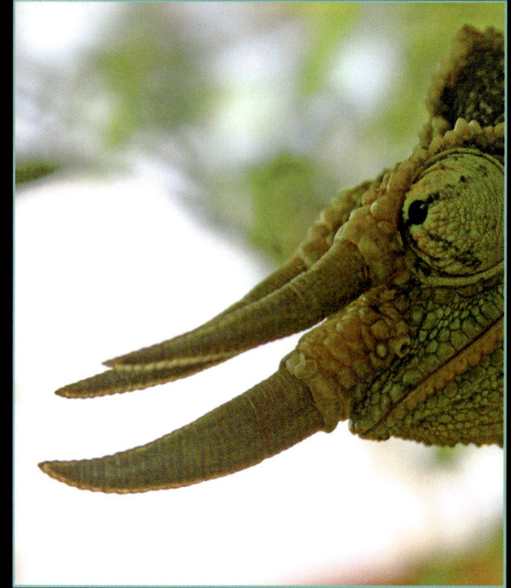

Alii

His horns have a slight green tint.

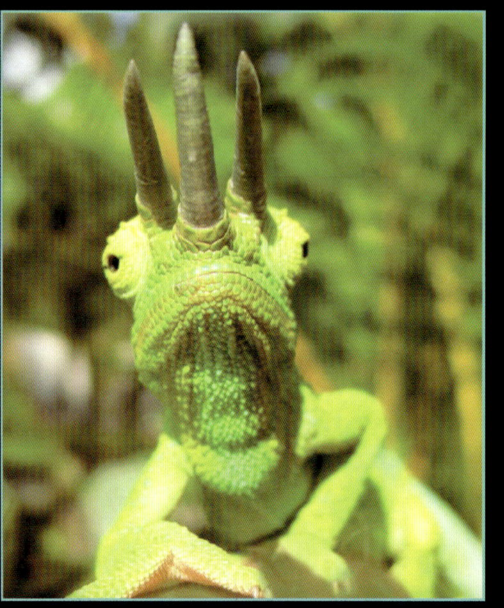

Spunk Bob

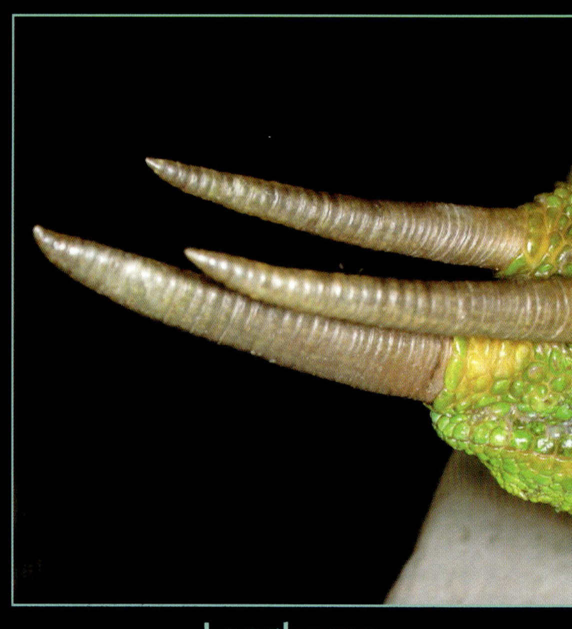

Longhorns

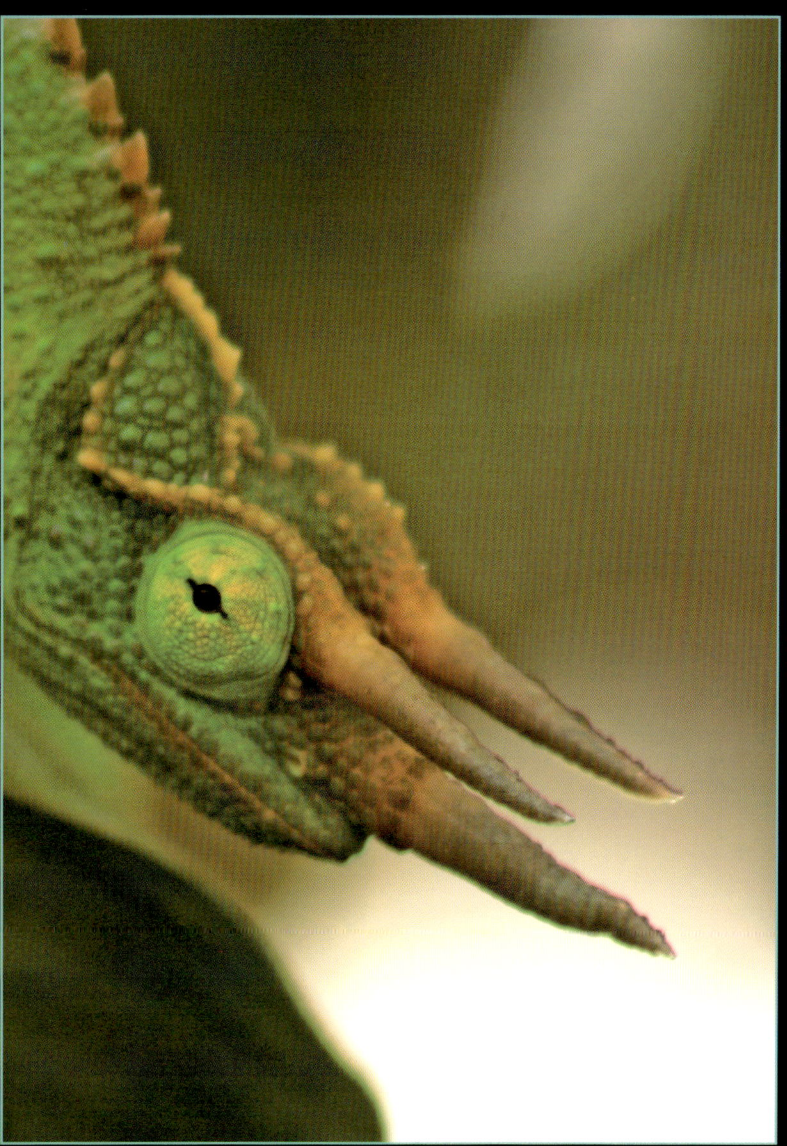

Pan

Every male's horns are different, which helps to identify individuals. Pan has a kink at the end of his rostral horn and yellow color at the bases.

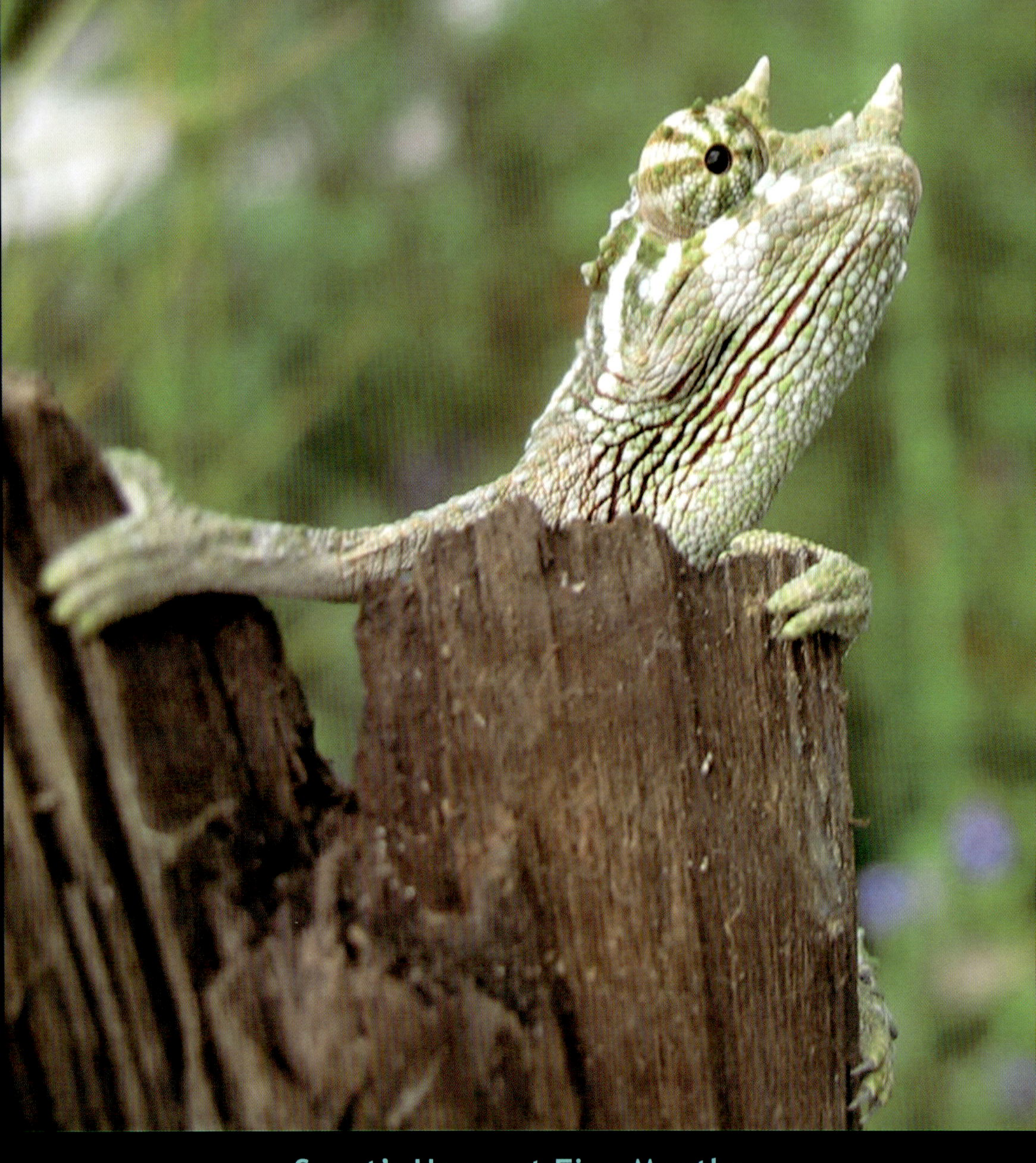

Scout's Horns at Five Months

Three Week Old Babies

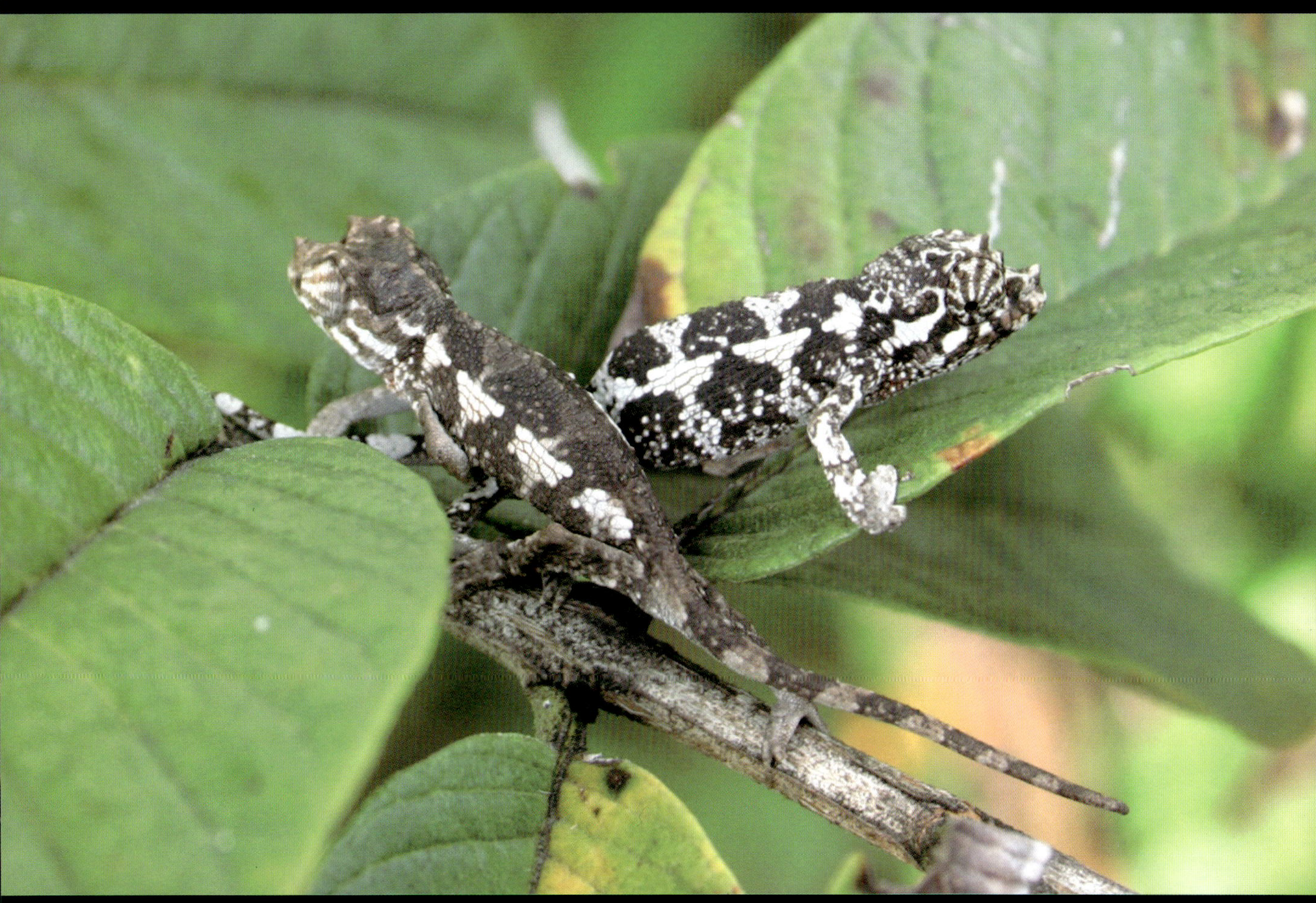

It's hard to tell males from females when they are babies. All of them have little nubbins on their heads. It becomes apparent which are males when they sprout horns at about three months. Females typically lack horns, although they may have a tiny, underdeveloped (rostral) horn. Males have a slightly thicker tail base.

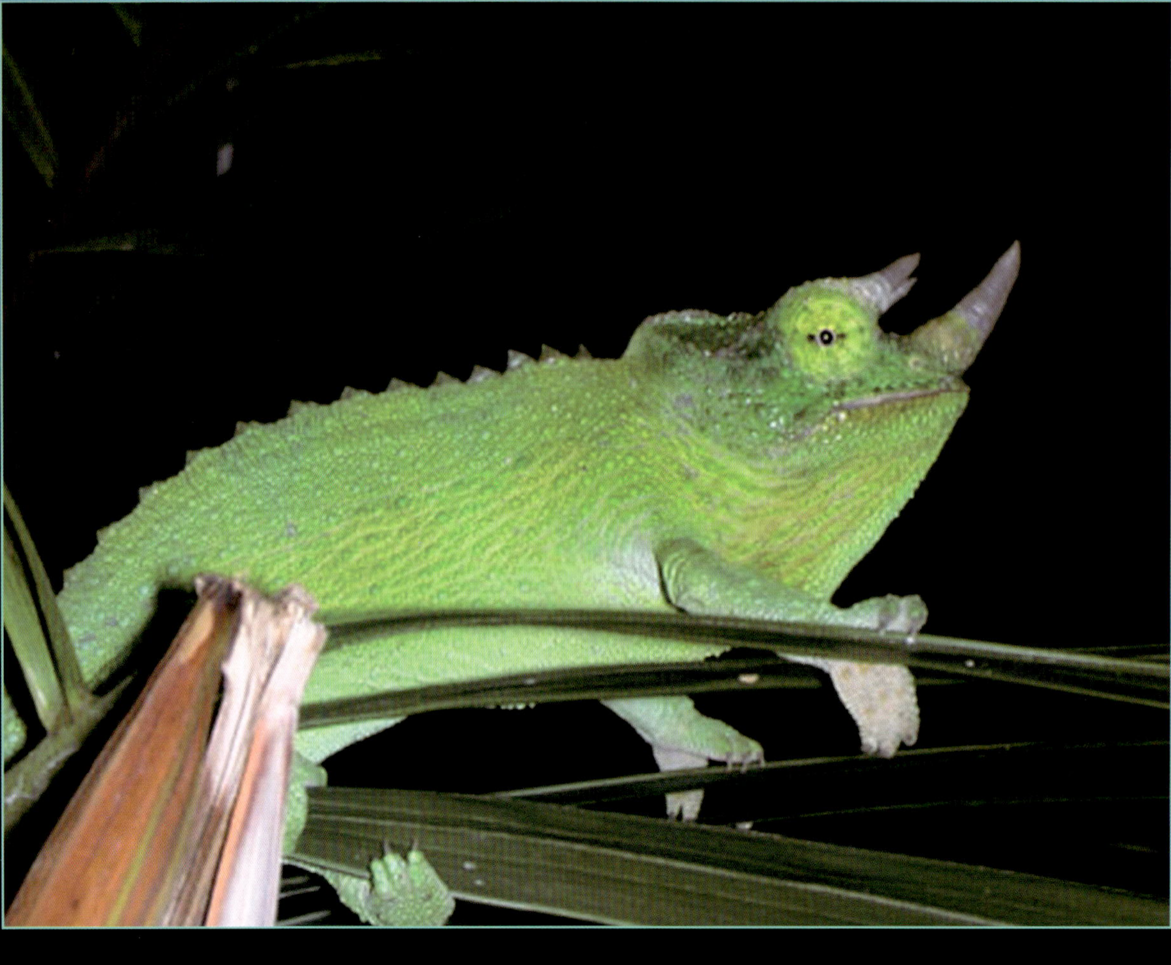

Tiny Dinosaurs

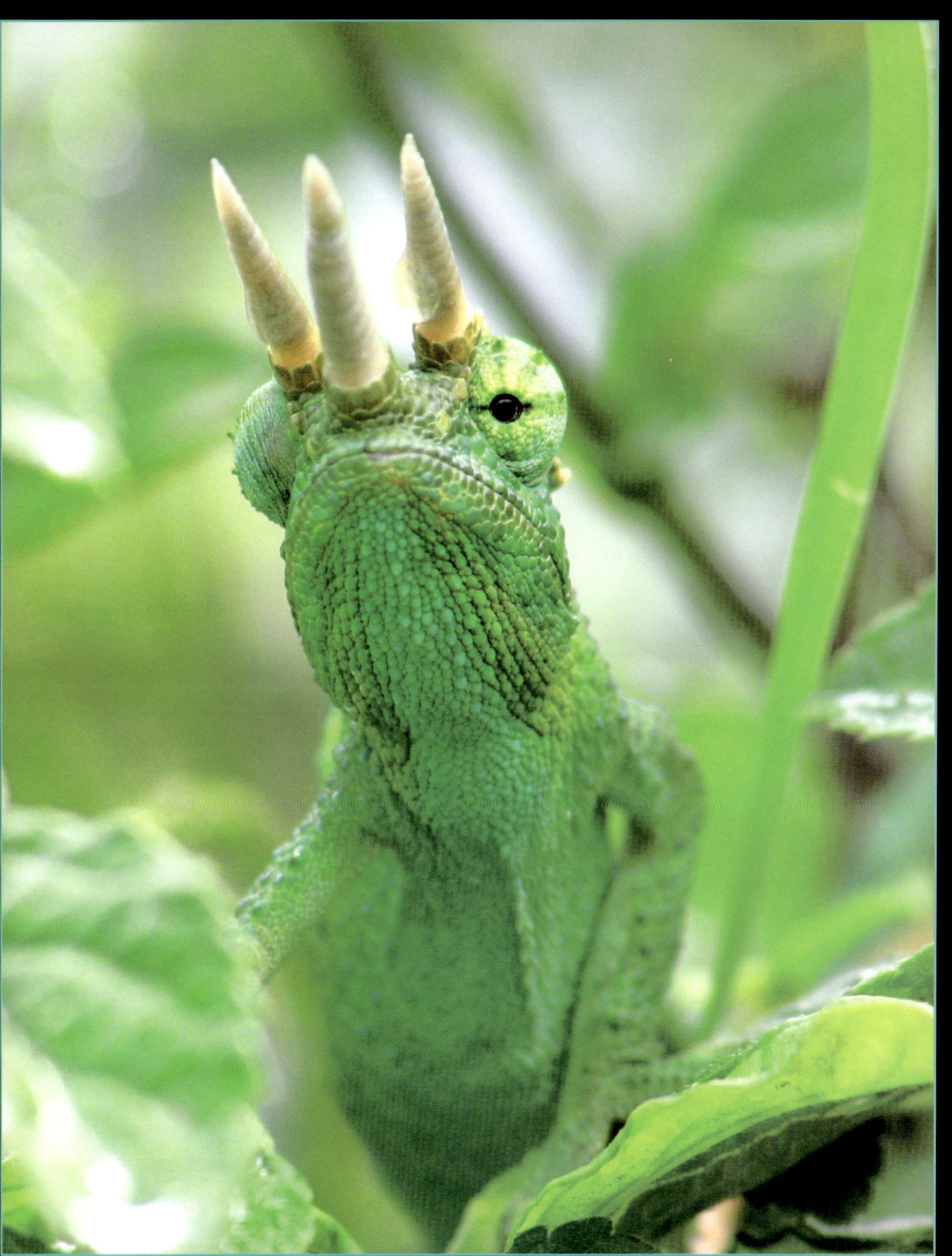

Rustling in the Palms Outside the Front Door

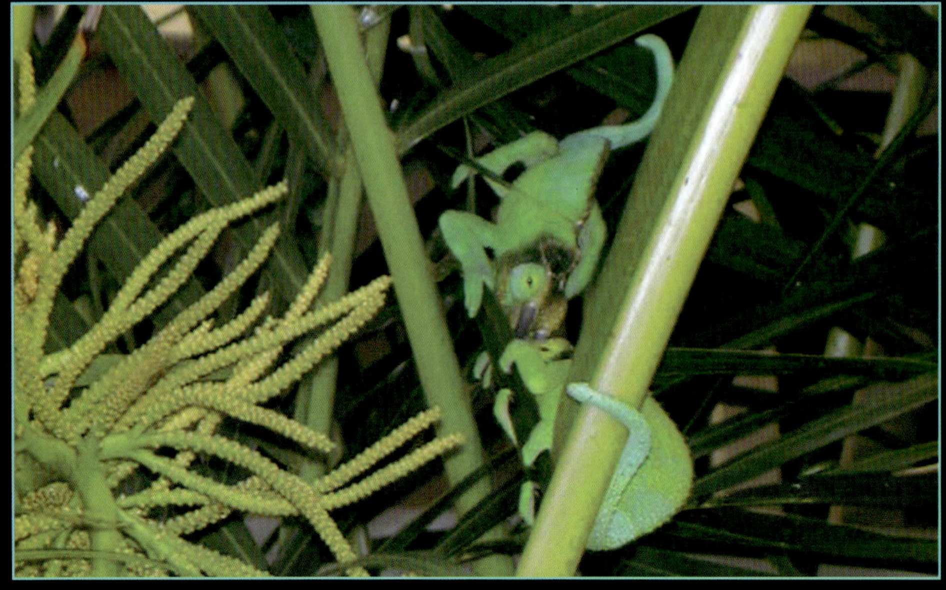

Horn-to-Horn Combat

Equal Opponents

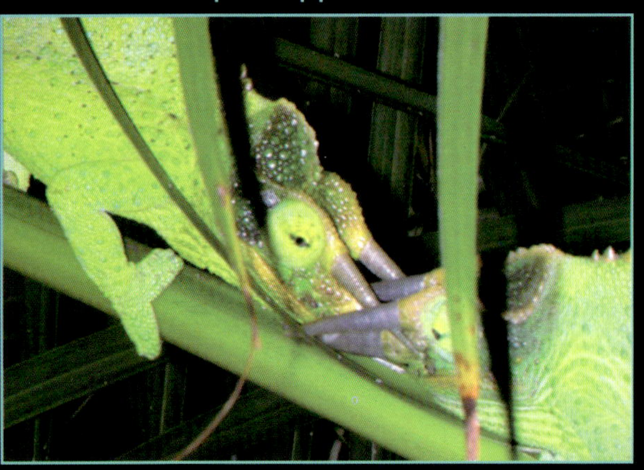

Adult males are territorial and will fight to protect their area, which may include a couple of trees or just one. Within a radius, there are usually several females and only one adult male, who is called the alpha male.

Close Match

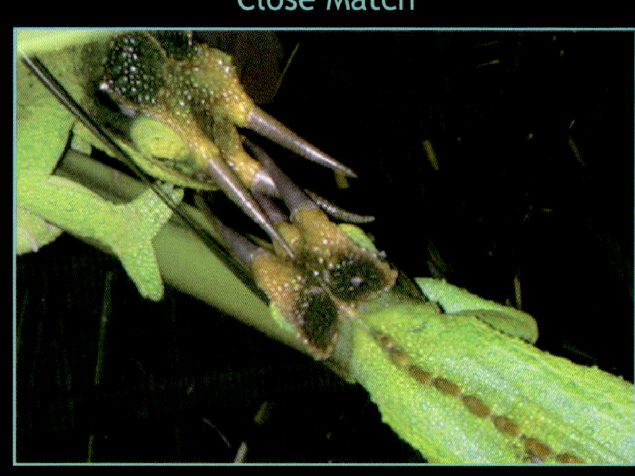

The resident alpha spotted another male and took action to defend his territory. Using his horns, he twisted the intruder until he forced him out of the Areca palm tree and onto the ground. There were no injuries.

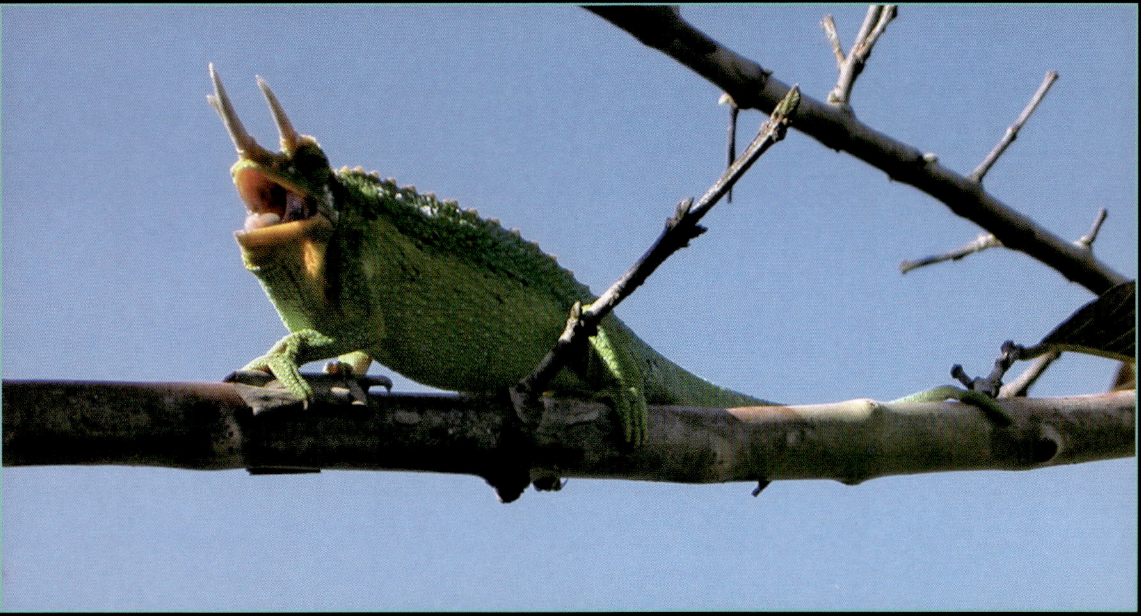

This male sports his brightest colors and looks as big as he can, when he sees a rival male in his territory. His throat is extended and he is fiercely gaping.

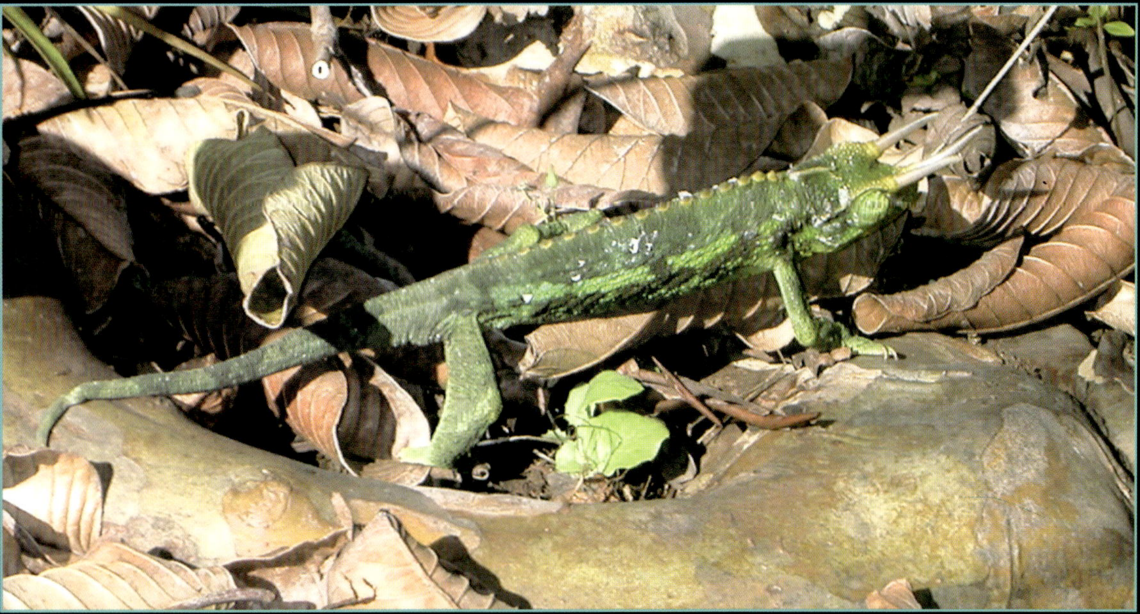

Sometimes, there is no fight at all, just displaying and posturing. The loser will indicate submission by exhibiting darker stress colors and making himself look as small as possible. This allows the smaller or weaker male to leave the area without risking injury.

Ipenda

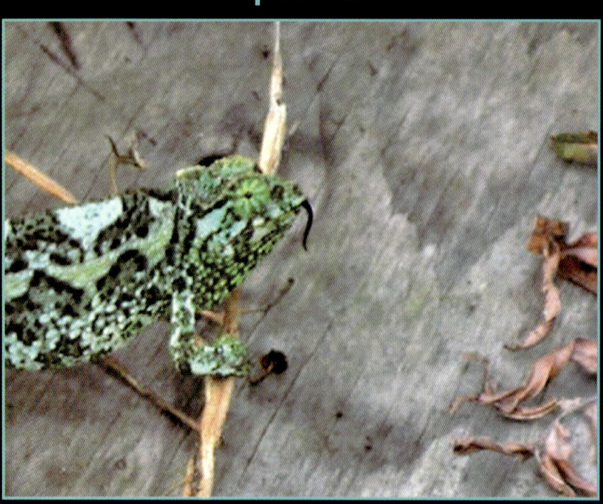

Named after the female chameleon in "Dragons of Namib," Ipenda came down from the Night Blooming Jasmine to eat a skink. The tail end is still poking out of her mouth (not for long though).

Spunk Bob

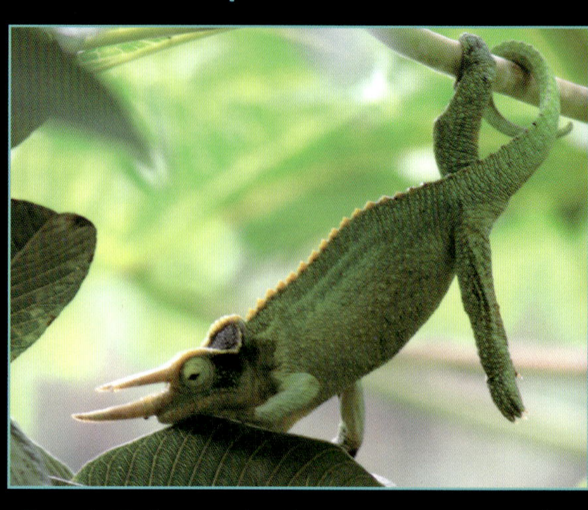

Spunk Bob was in the guava tree and had been watching. He climbed down to get to her as fast as he could, stopping only to look over, while bobbing, shaking and nodding his head in a dynamic courtship display.

Man on a Mission

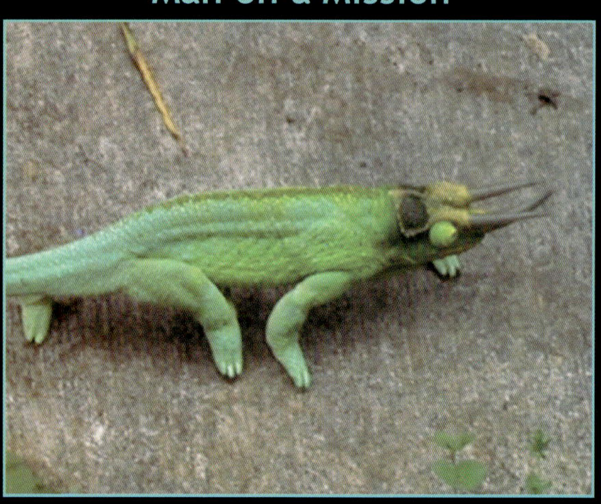

He passed right in front of Matt and me on his way to meet her. The chameleon's gait is very distinctive and does not resemble that of any other lizard. They are slow, yet deliberate, cautiously hesitant with each step. I call it the Tai Chi Mambo.

Courting Ipenda

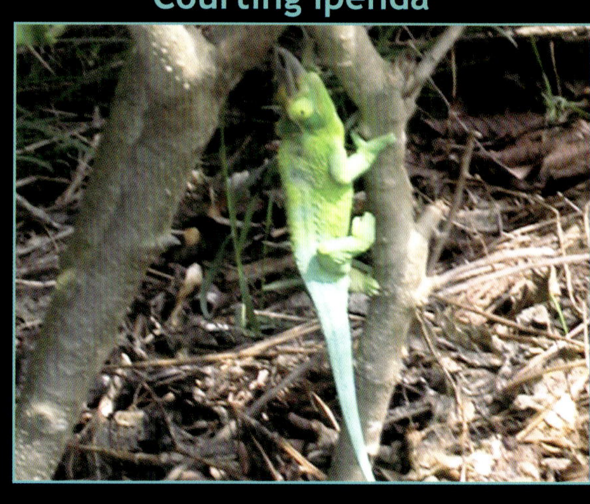

He was wearing his best colors. She was not receptive, however. He continued to enthusiastically bob his head. After awhile, with no green light from her, he went back to the ground, but then without missing a beat, he climbed right back up to check on her again.

Ipenda and Spunk Bob

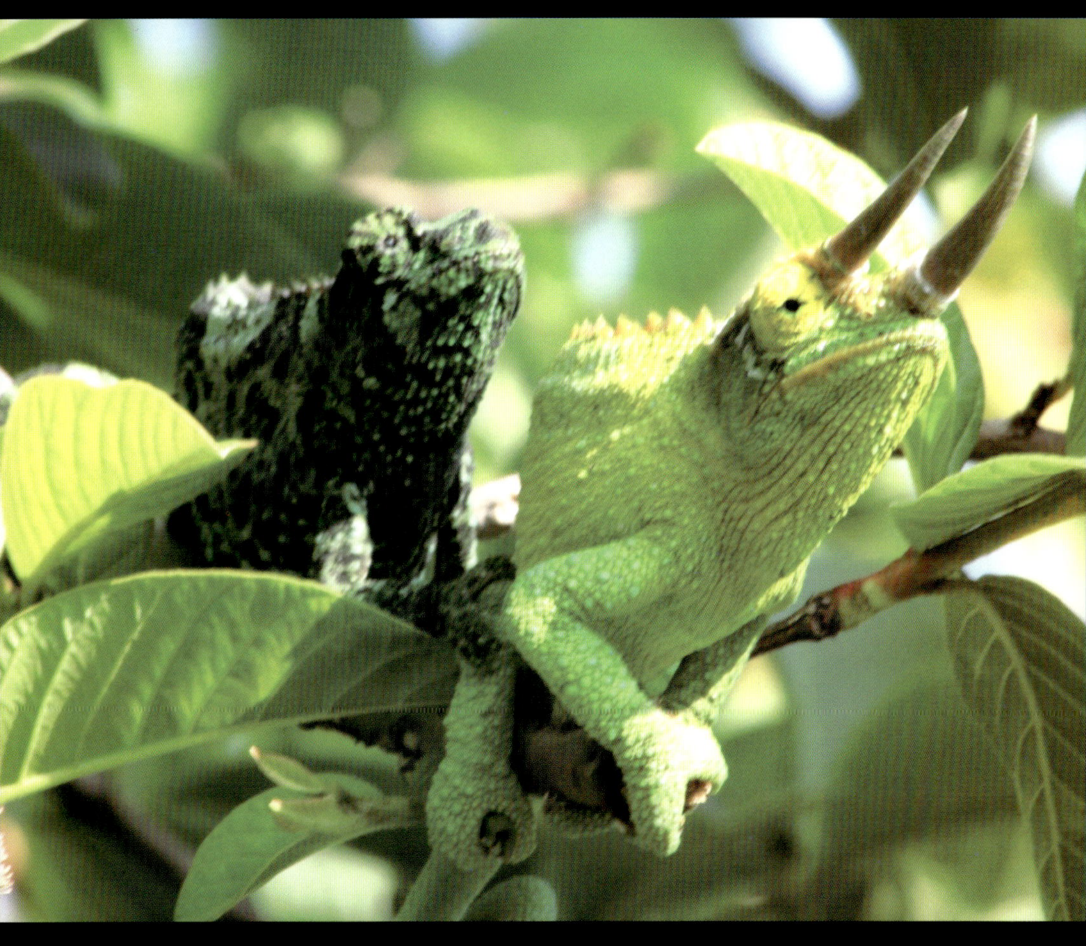

They remained close for a few weeks, then he returned to his tree, but kept an eye on her. He continued to pursue her regularly and she ended up moving to his place in the guava tree.

She Said No!

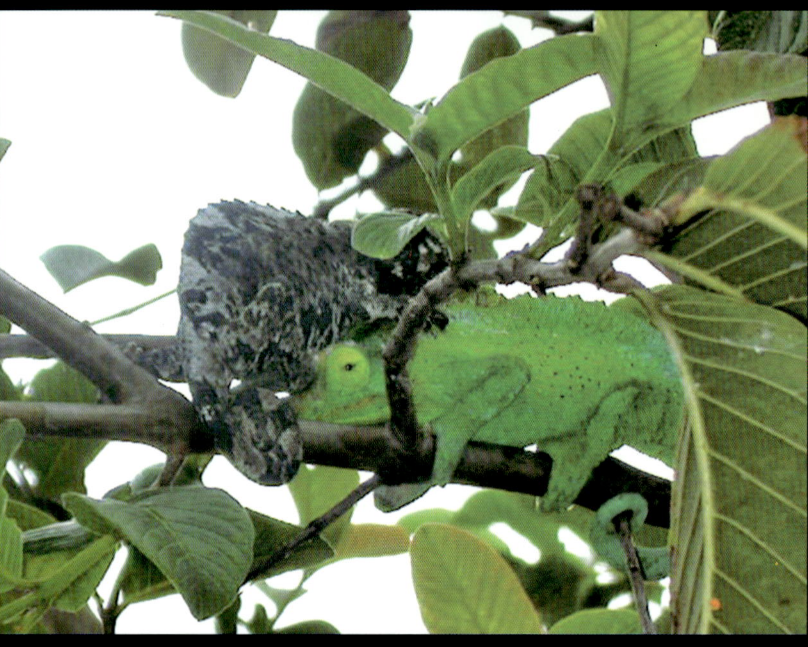

Ipenda is letting Spunk Bob know she is not in the mood by sitting on his head. She looks stressed and dark as he continues to display his bright colors.

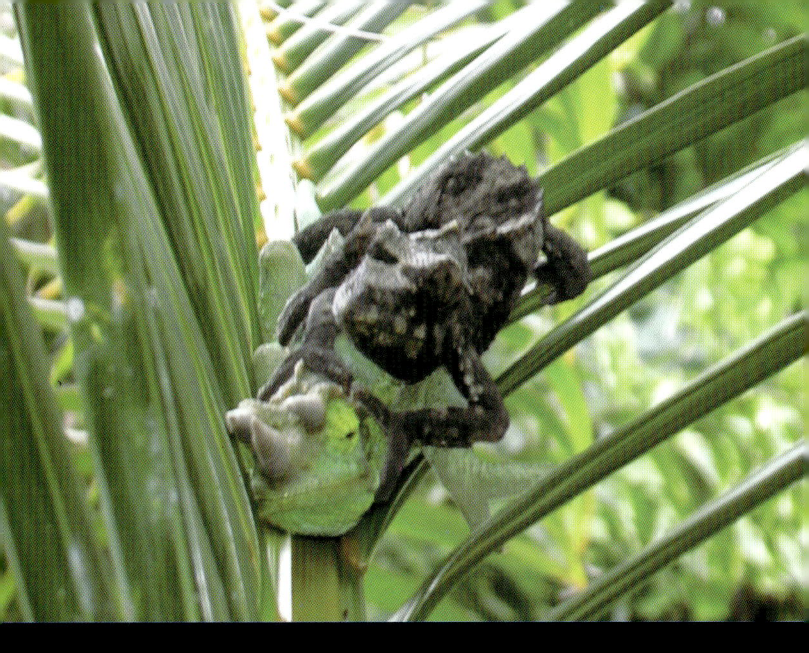

This is another case of a female making it clear she is not receptive (as she appears to wring his neck). Strangely, he does not look as though he minds.

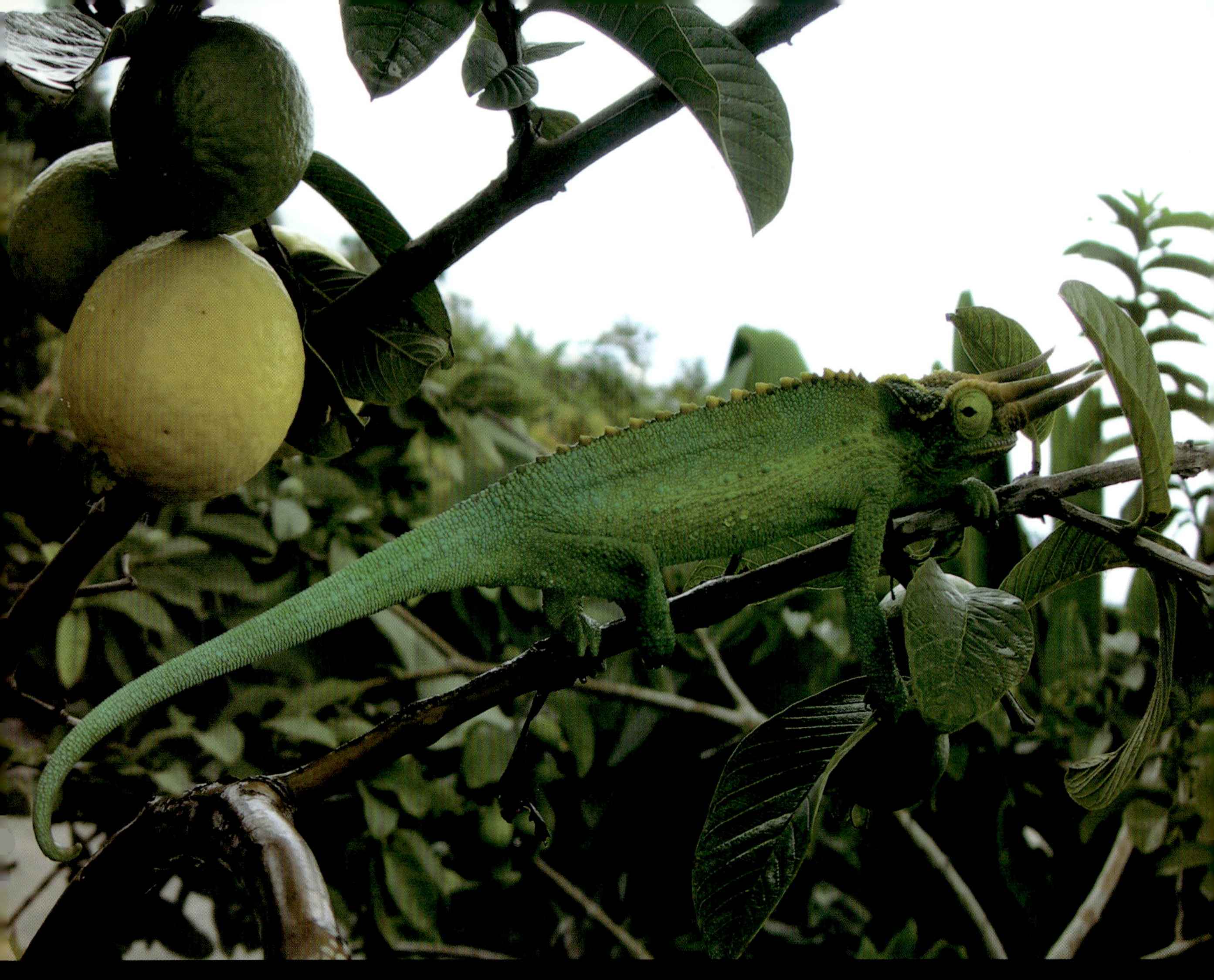

It's a Lizard's Life

Chameleons have a relatively short life span, but may live for a decade under the right circumstances.

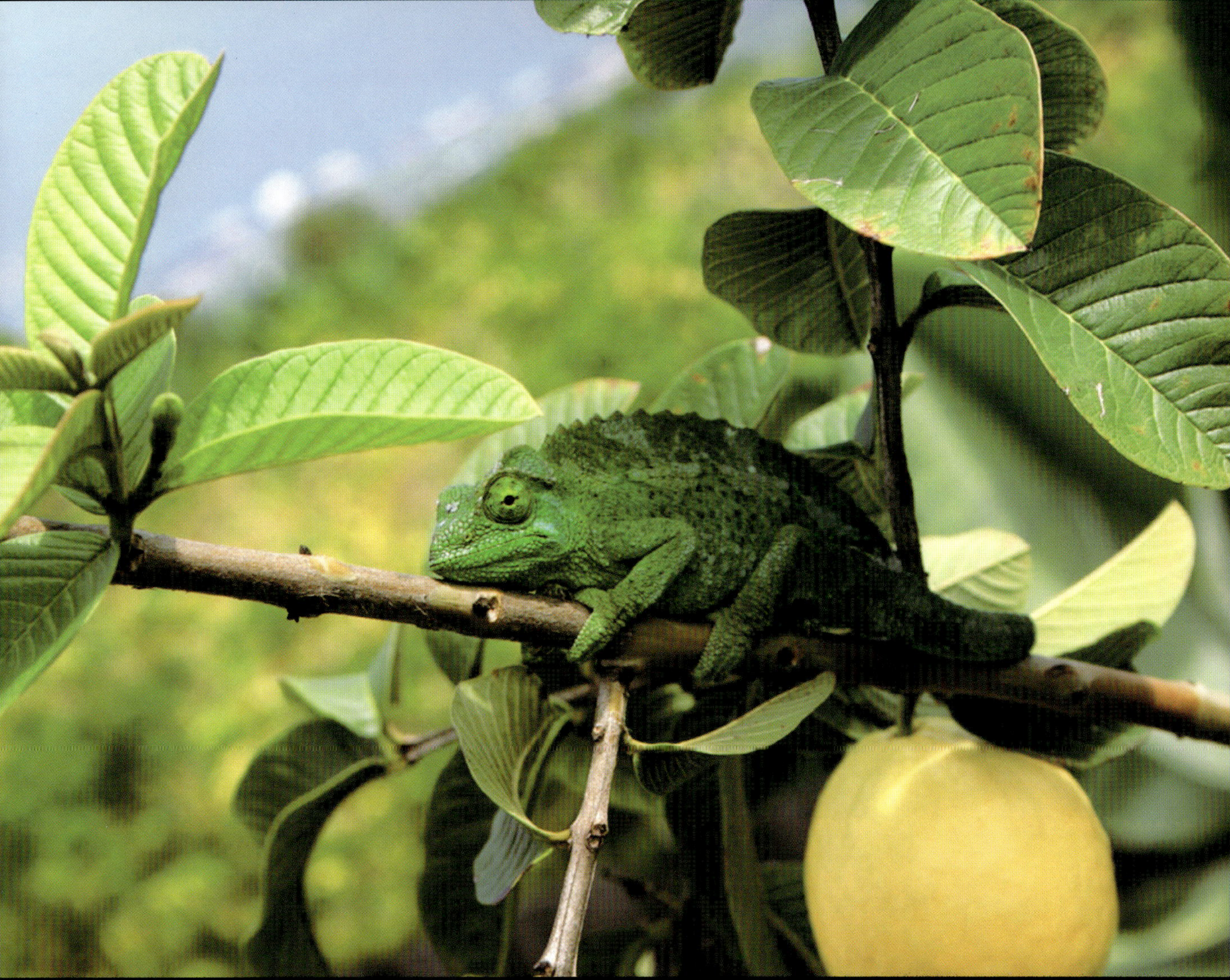

Glorious Day in the Guava Tree

The guava tree provides ideal living conditions. A variety of insects are attracted to the fruits and blossoms. The fallen fruit draws fruit flies for the neonates.

One Minute Old

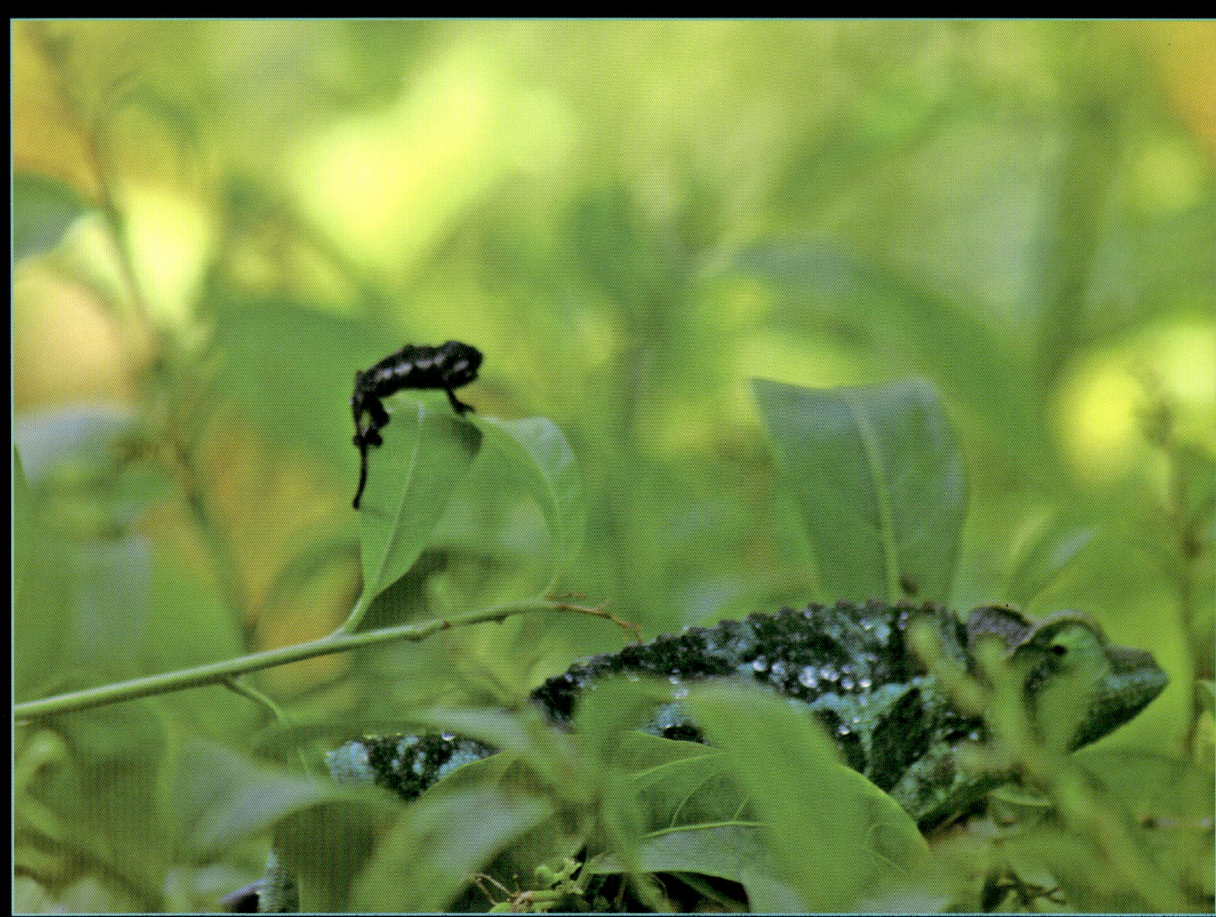

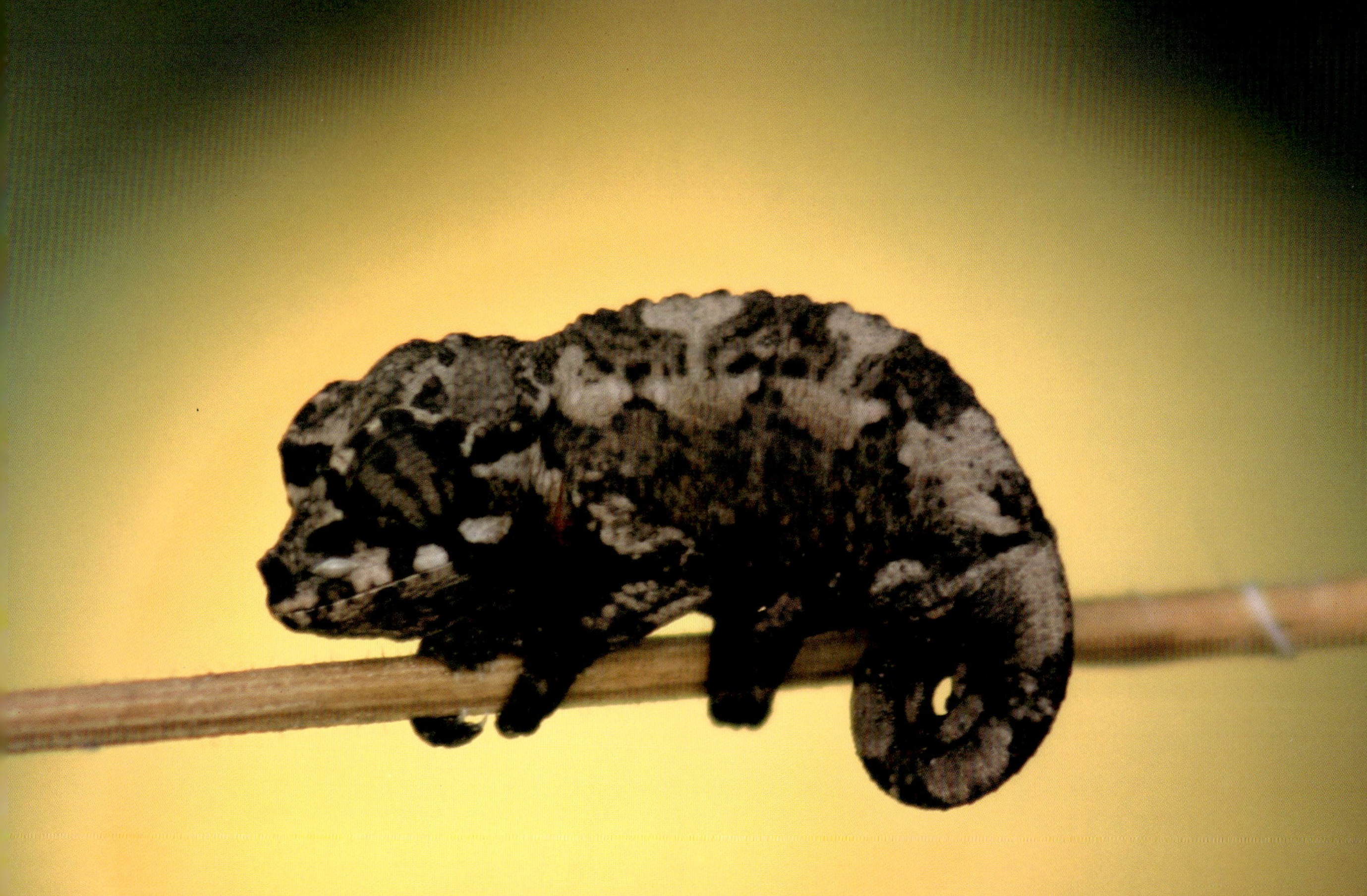

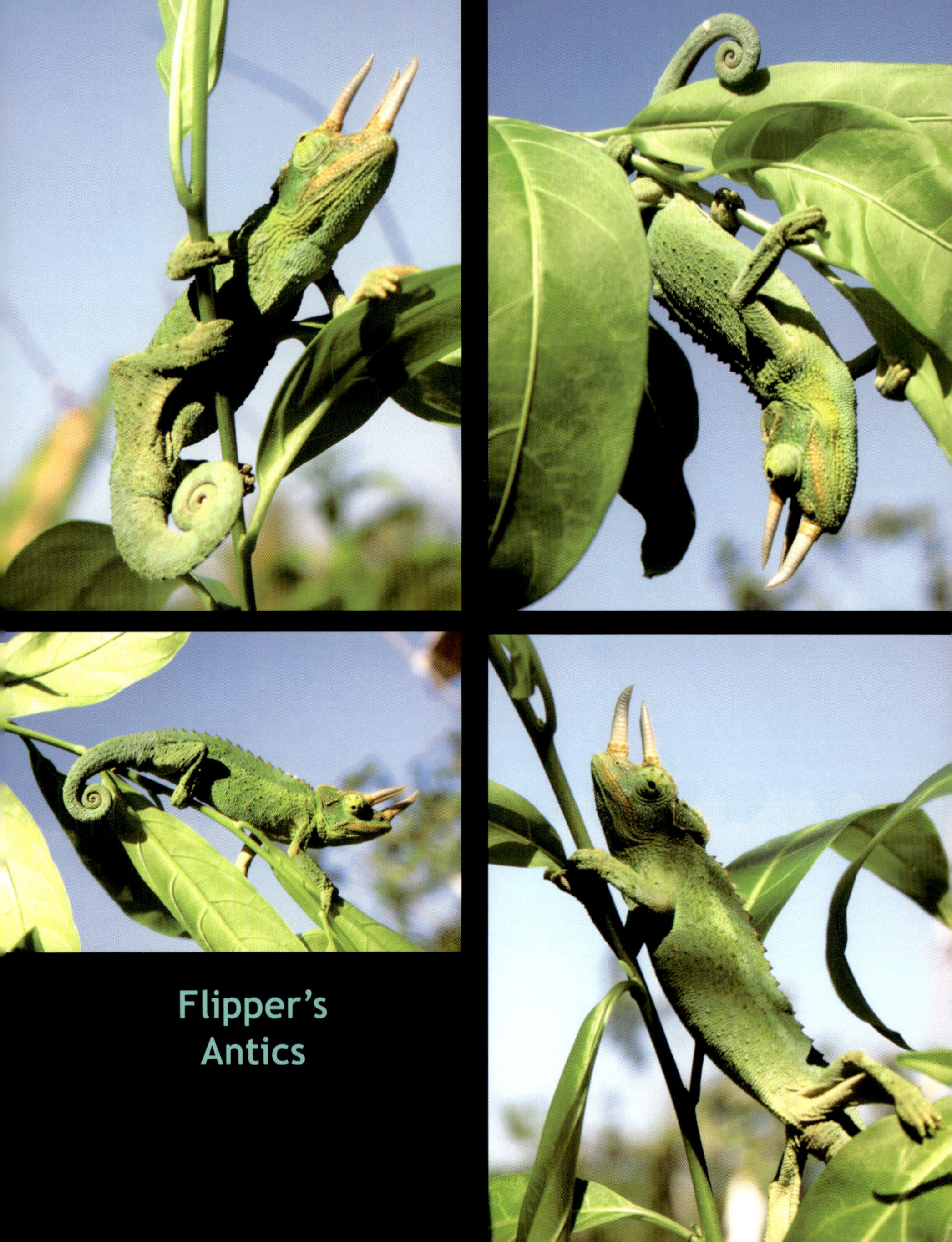

Flipper's Antics

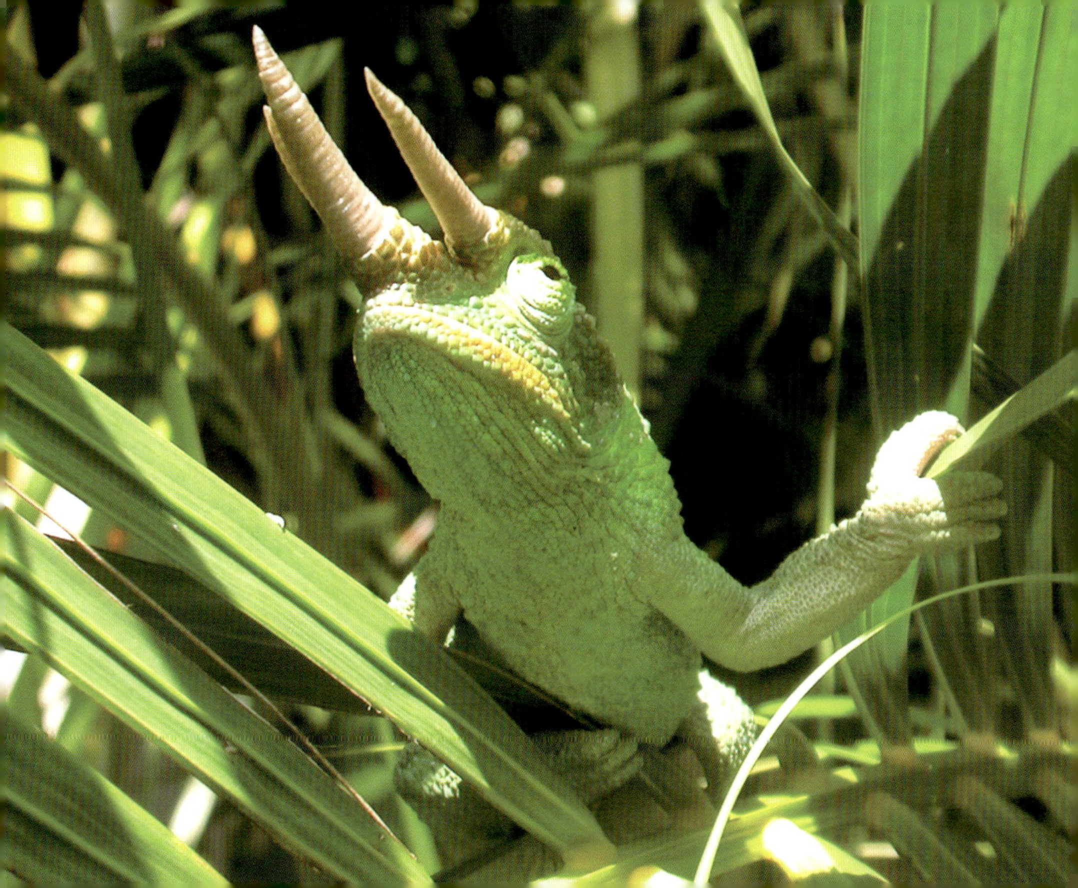

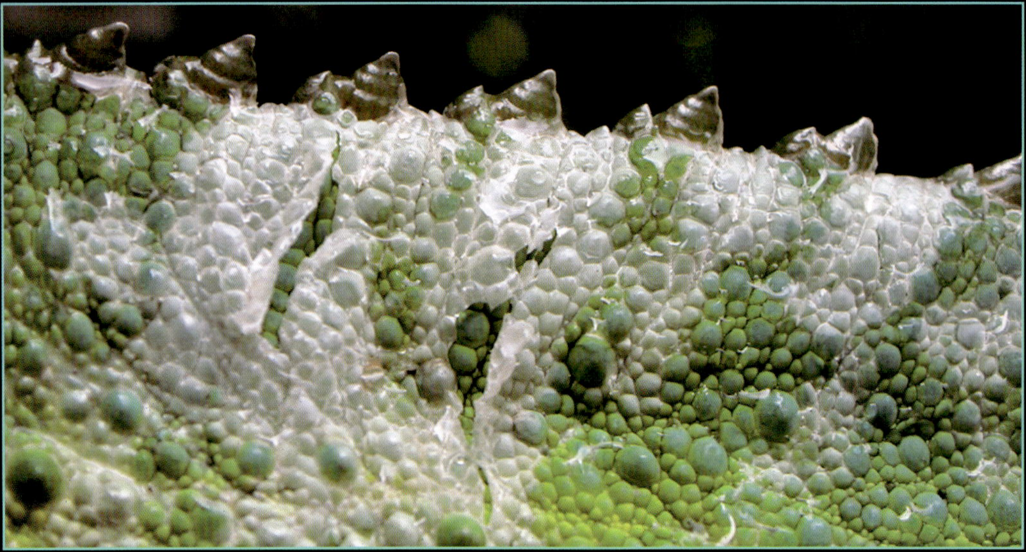

Dorsal Majesty

Shedding

During a shed, the chameleon rubs against branches to remove the dead skin

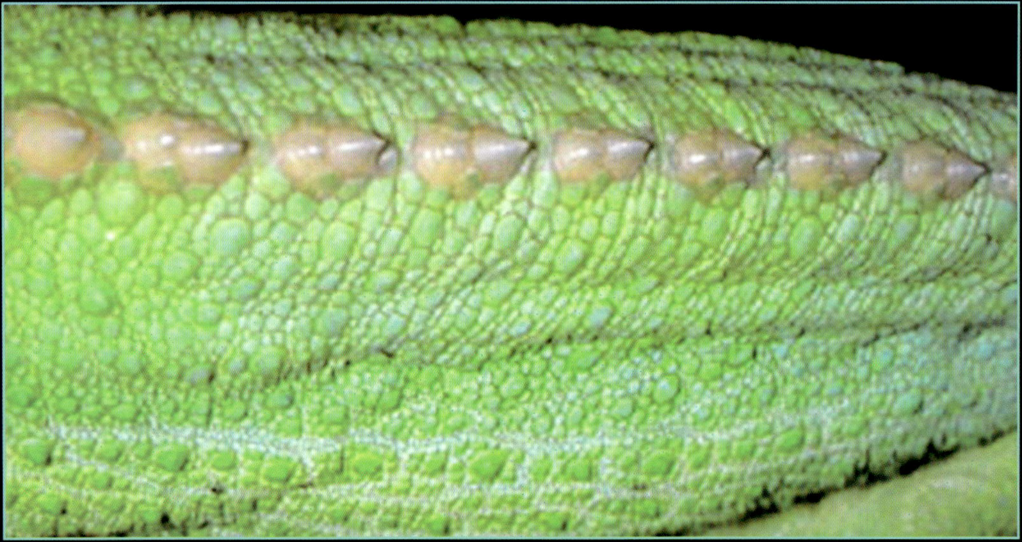

After the Shed

Rough spots disappear, leaving a flawless and healthy appearance.

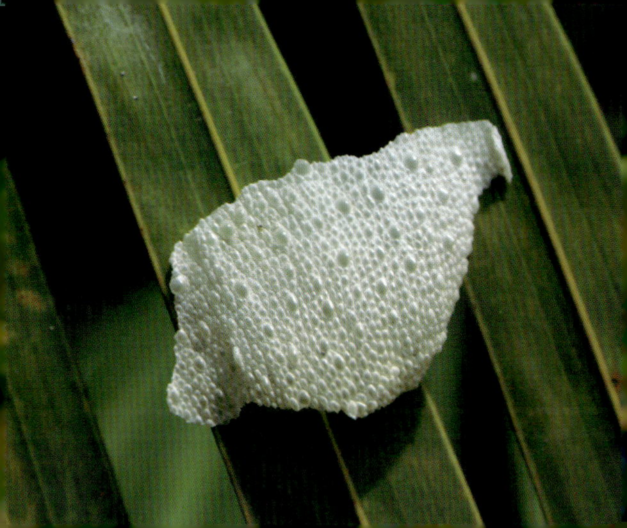

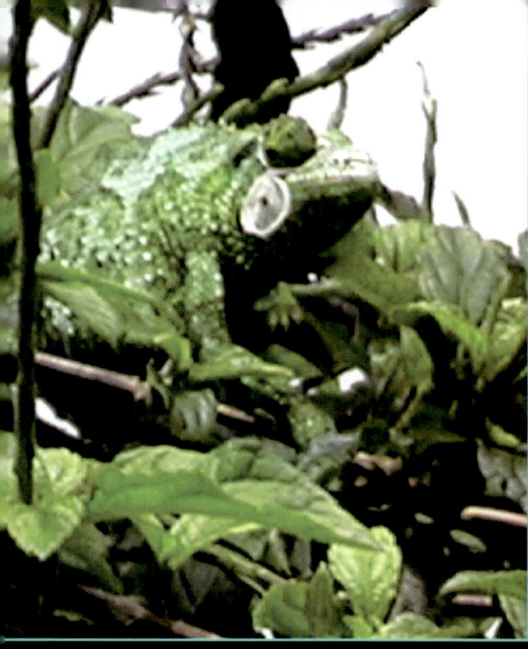

Now You See it, Now You Don't

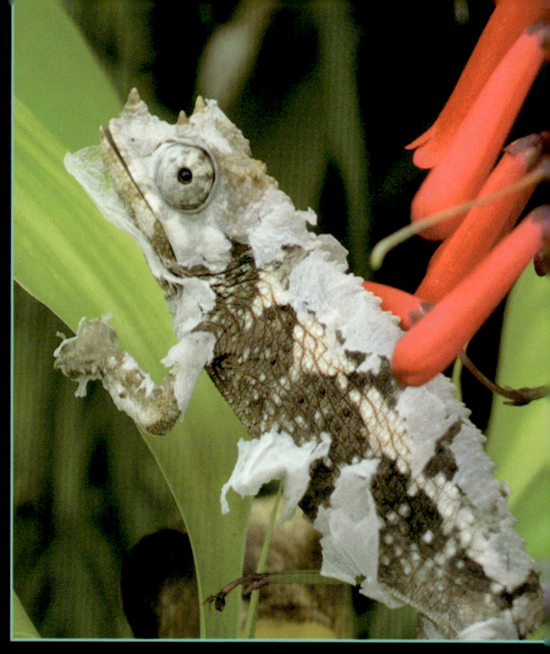

Bustin' Out All Over

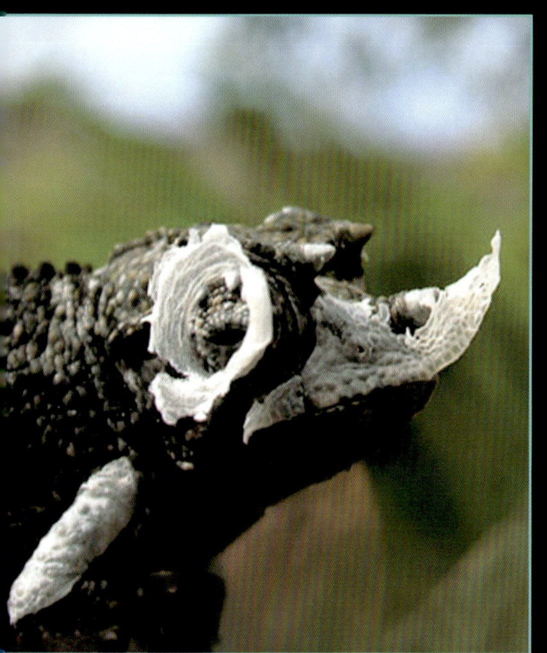

Mu's Impression of a Rhinoceros

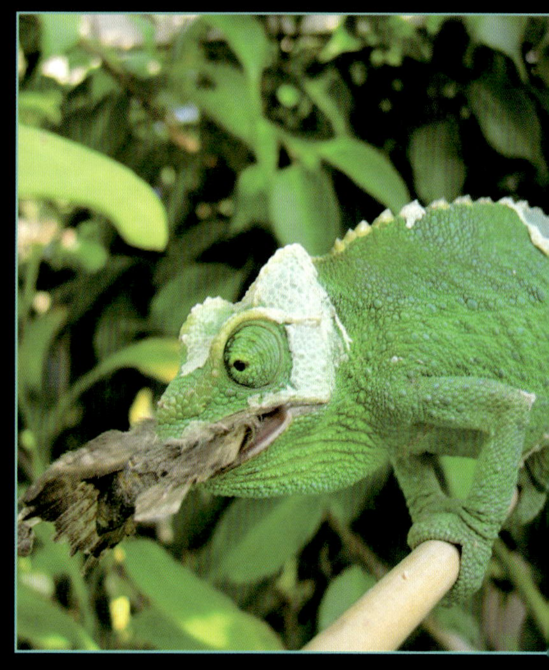

Wearing a Bonnet at Dinnertime

She Doesn't Look Her Best, But that's OK With Him

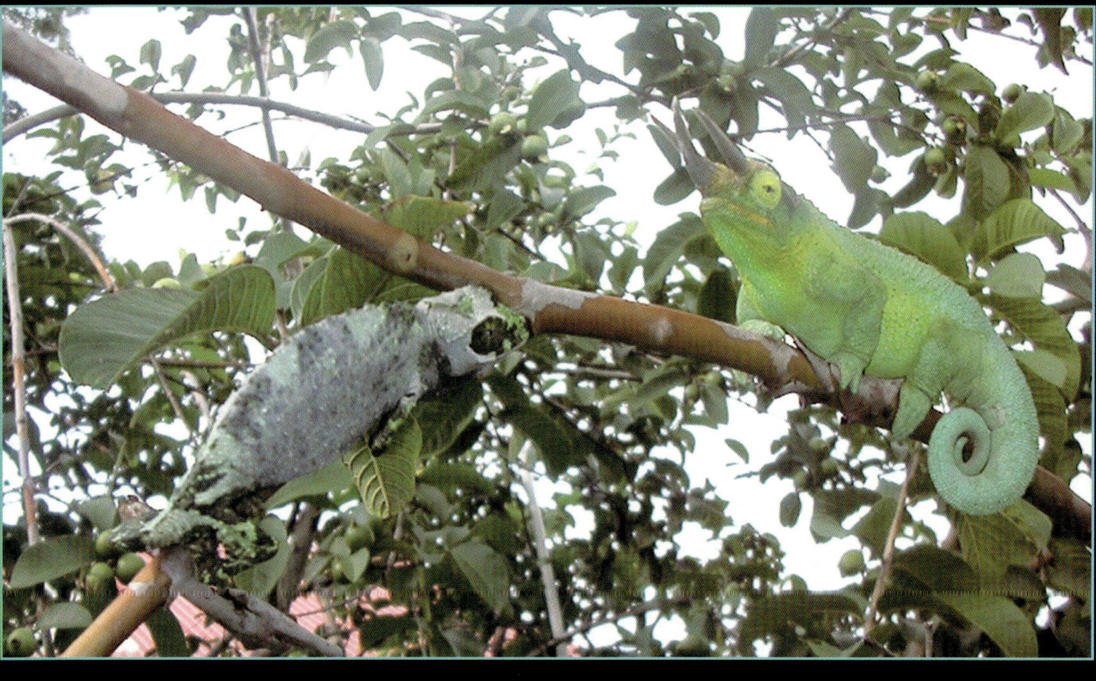

Shedding Female with Male

Alii Swinging

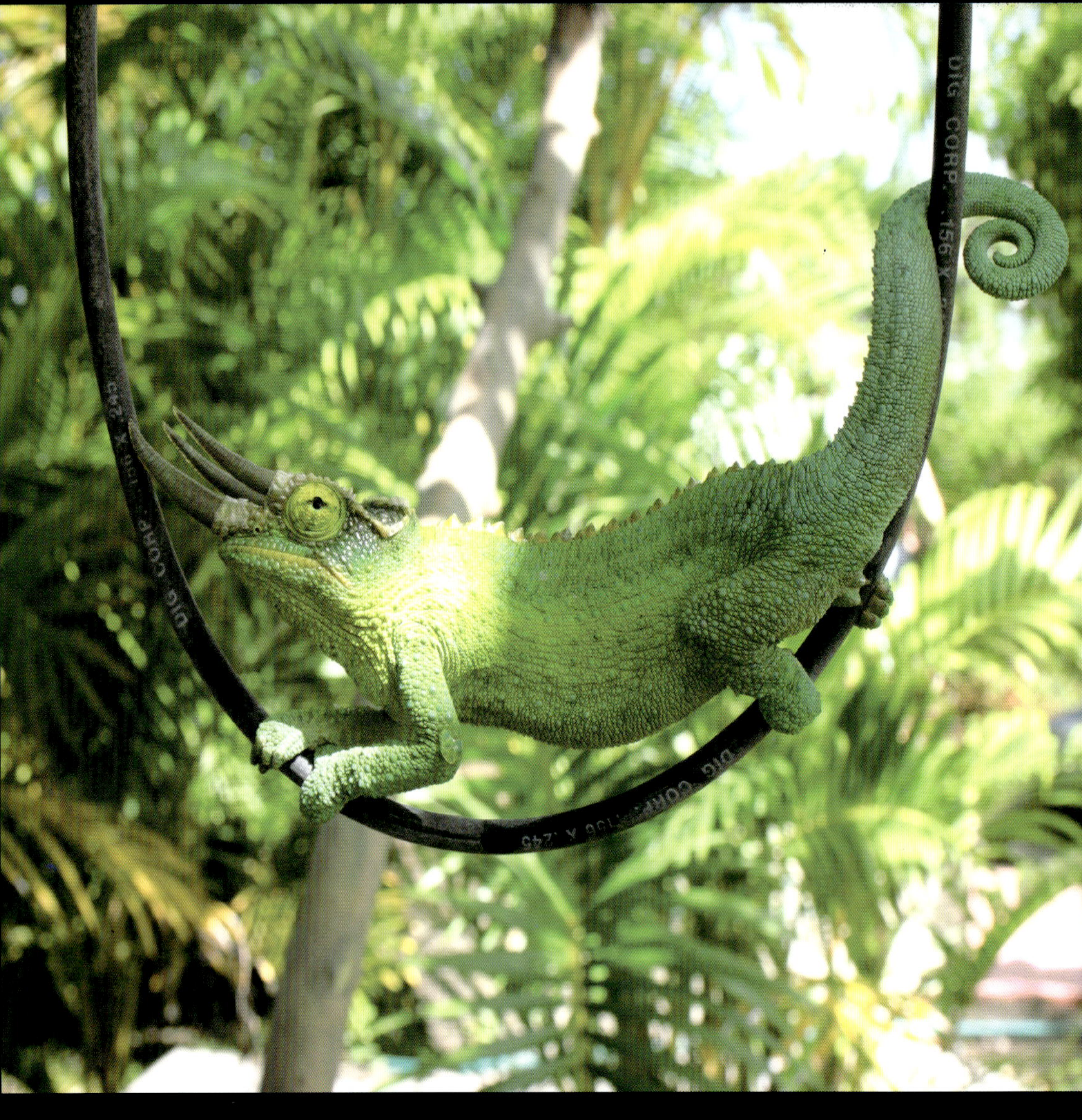

Chameleons treat the watering tube in the garden as if it was natural habitat. It serves as a tubular highway or a tightrope to get from point A to point B. Like some monkeys, they have a prehensile tail that can be used as a fifth limb.

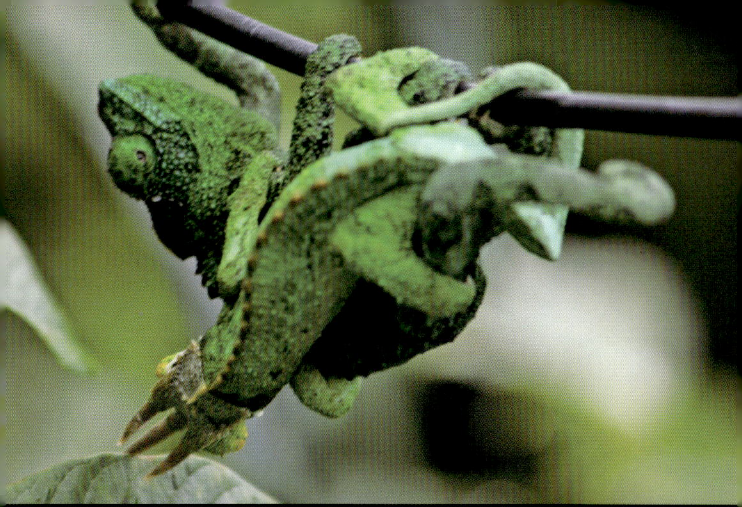

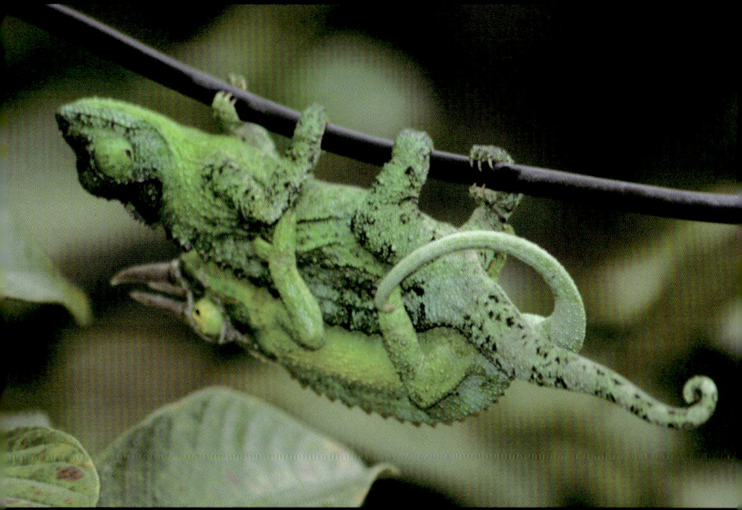

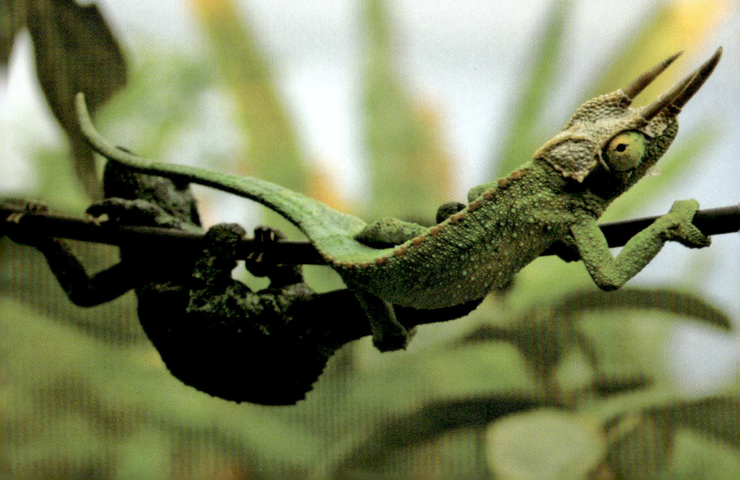

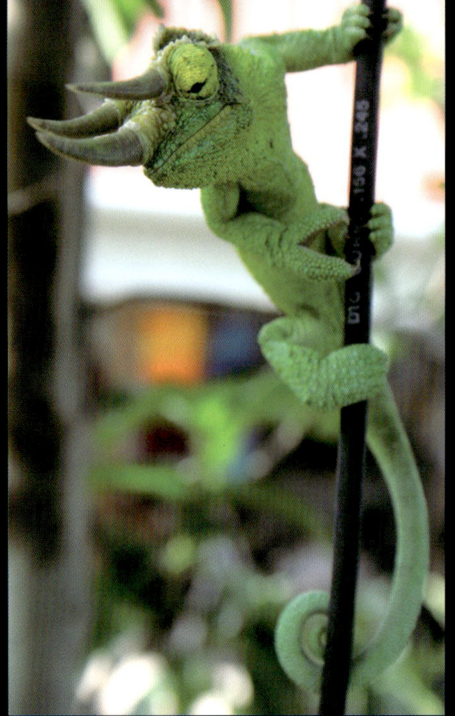

The front feet have two toes on the outside and three on the inside.

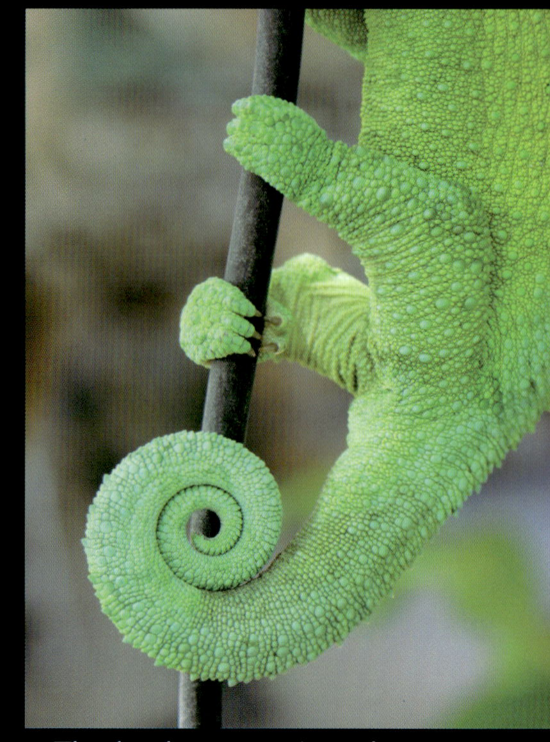

The back set are just the opposite with three toes on the outside.

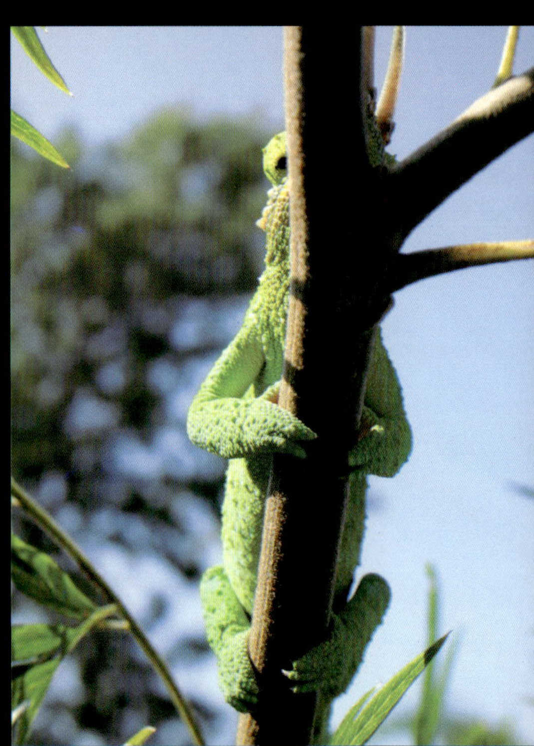

A healthy chameleon has a strong grip.

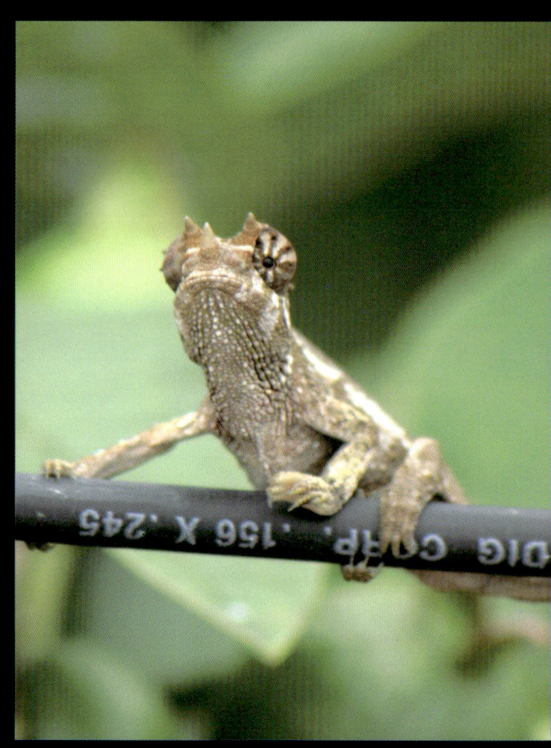

They have incredible balance and dexterity.

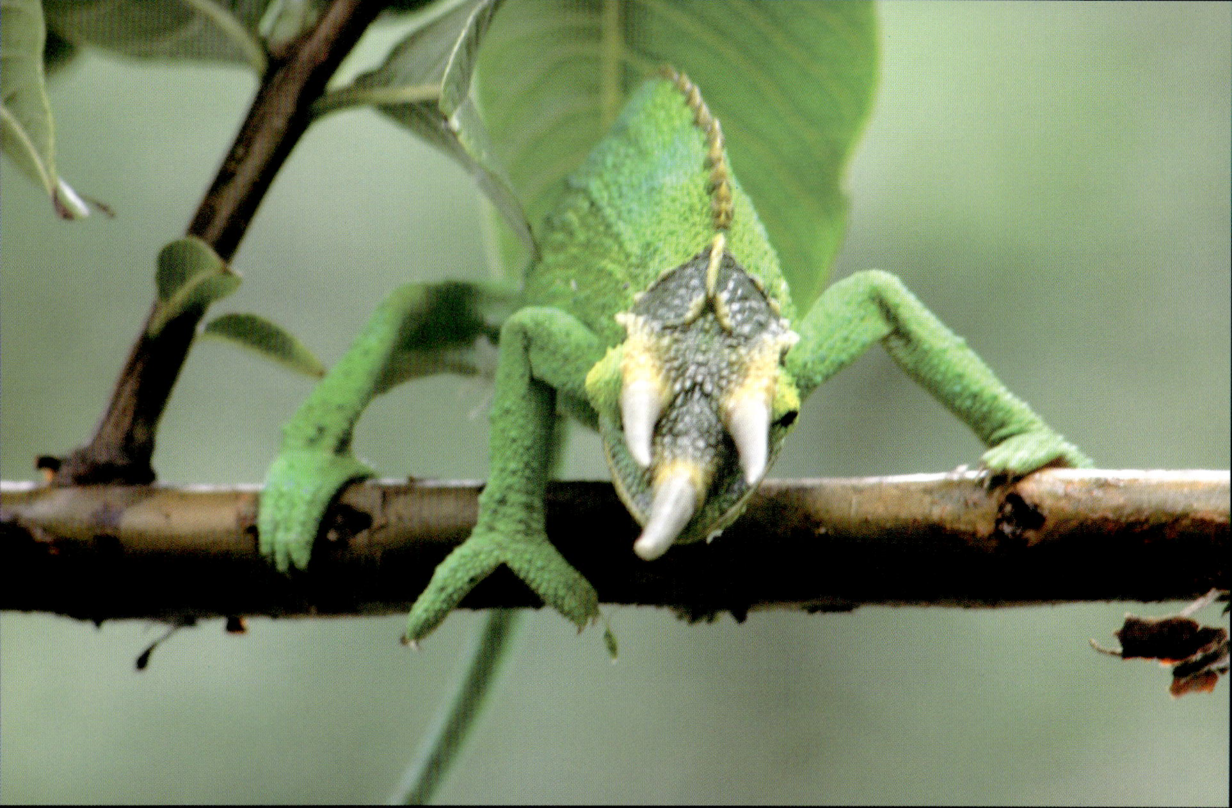

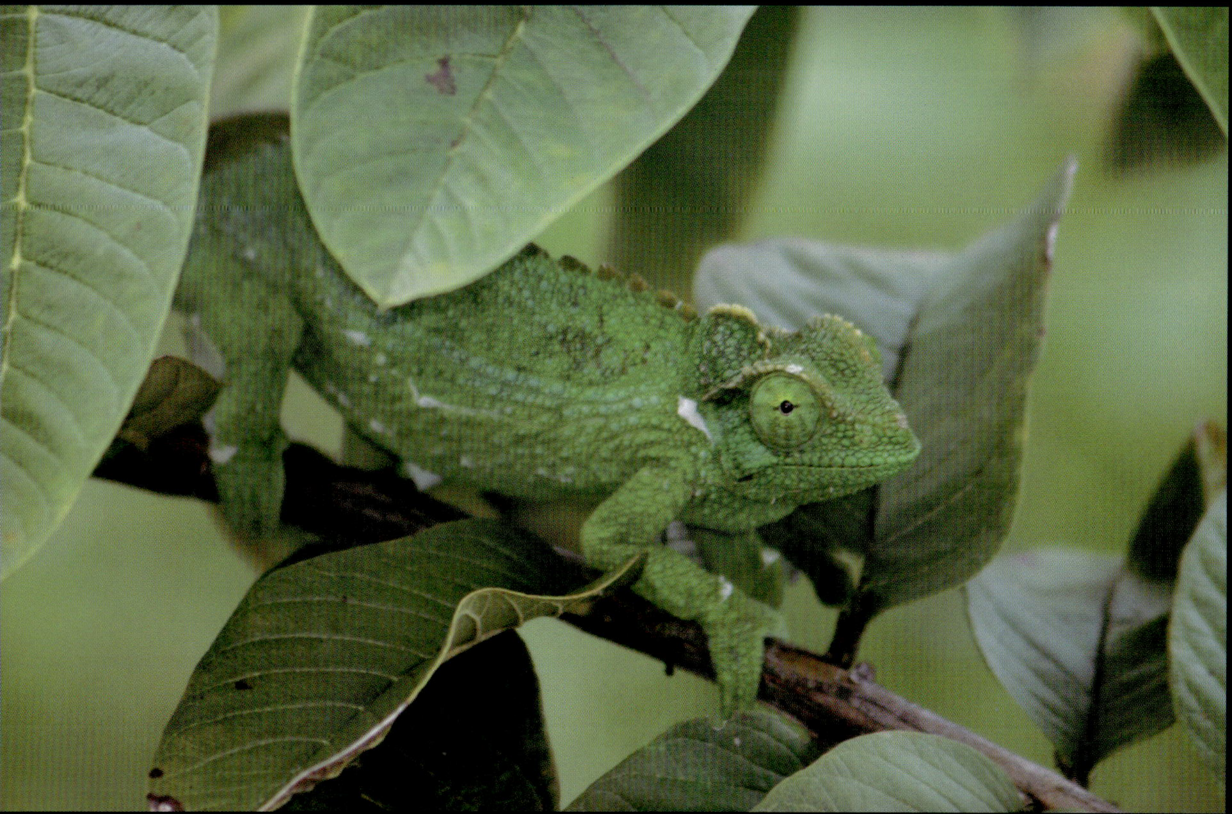

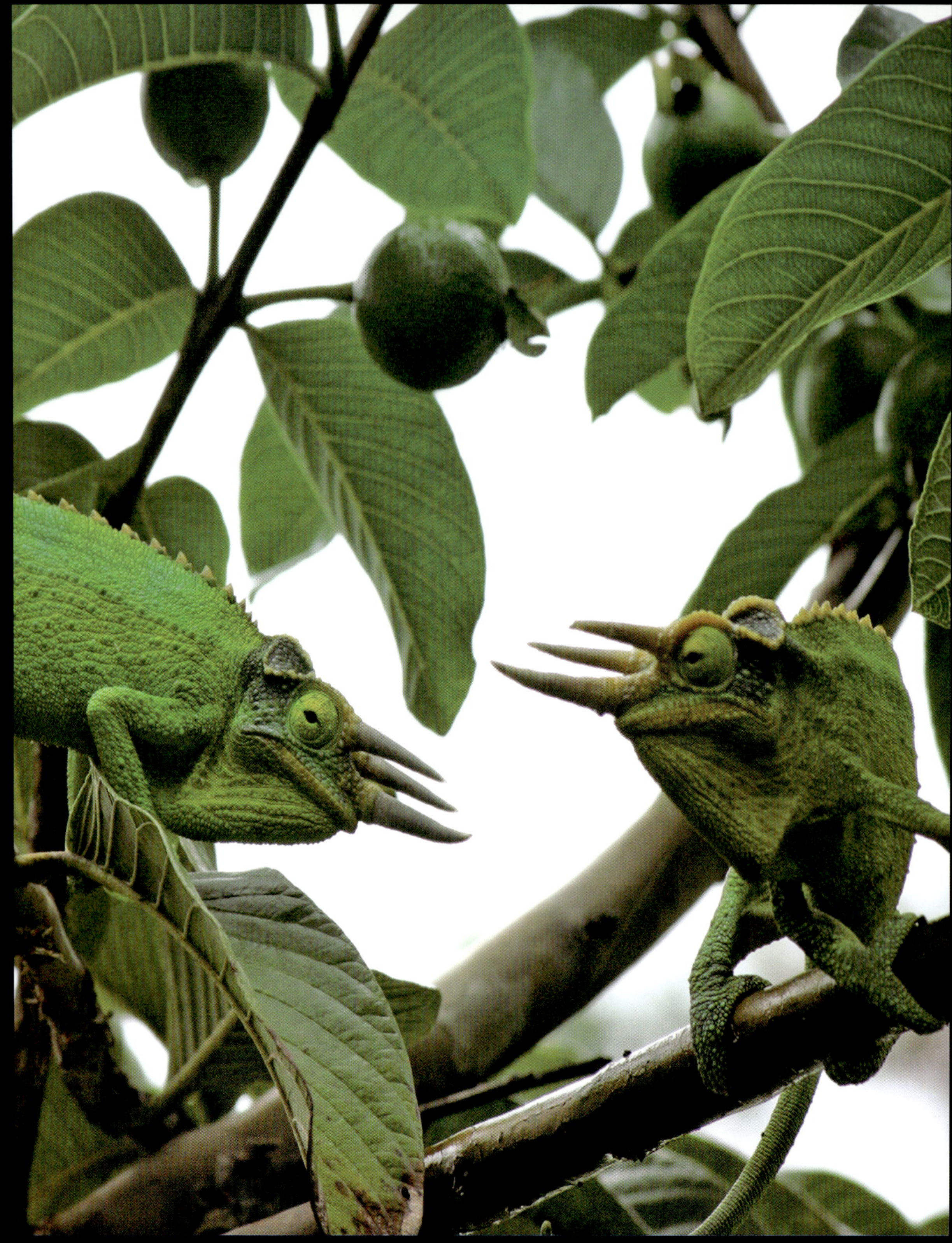

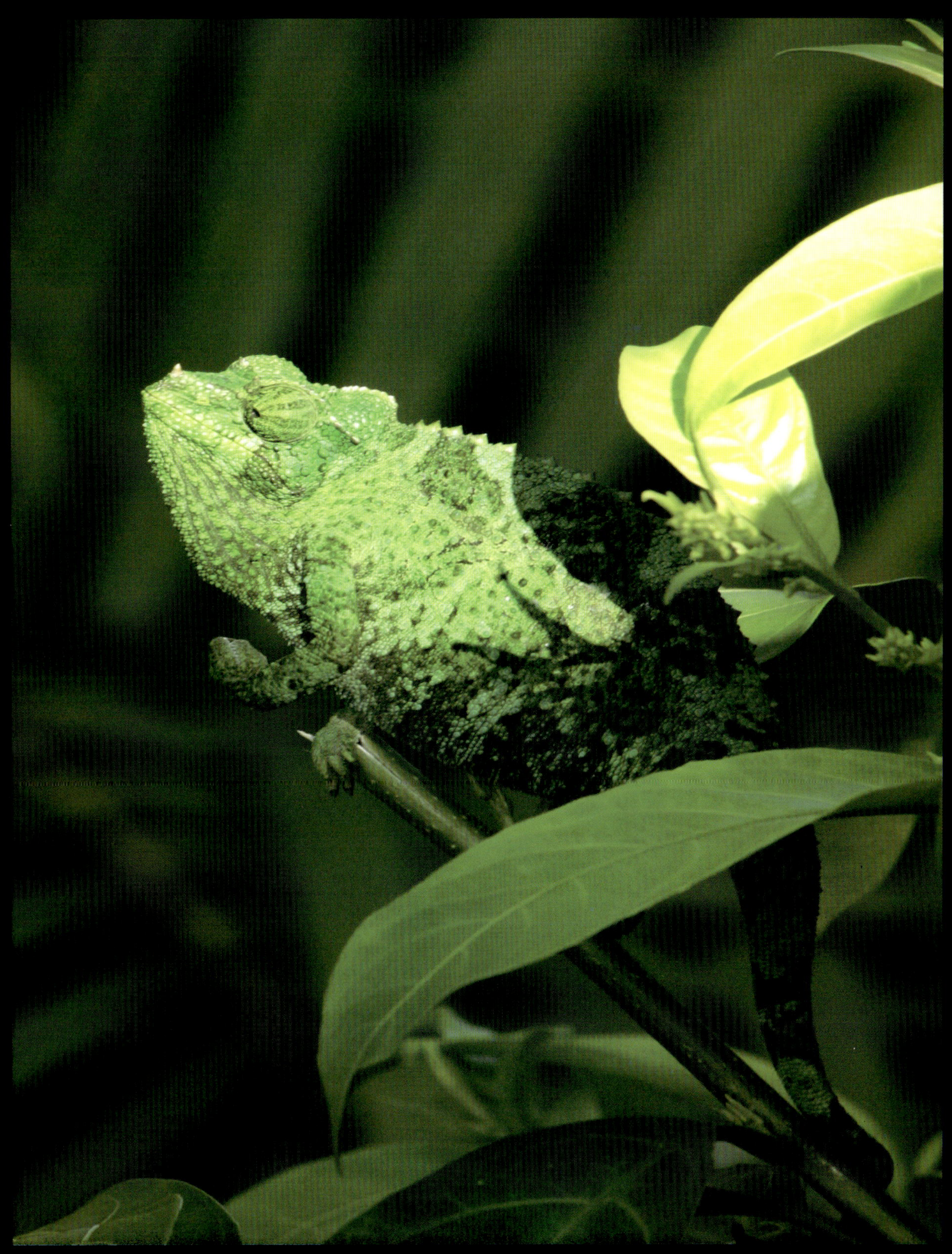

Chameleon Eyes

From the time they are born, chameleons have a sunburst pattern on each eye turret and as they mature it may disappear completely or reappear occasionally with skin variations.

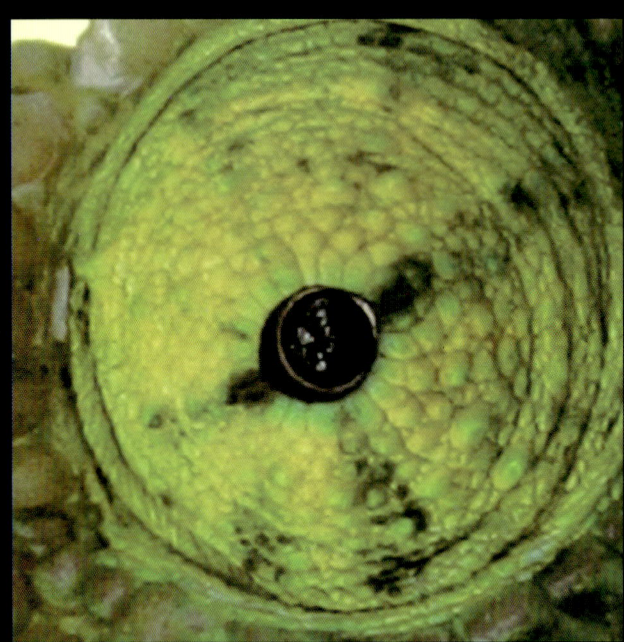

Chameleons are vulnerable to predators, such as cats, rats, humans or even ants. They don't have ears, though they can detect vibrations. They have no vocal chords. Their bite is benign and they move slowly. Their strongest defense mechanism is their vision, which serves as an early warning system.

The eyes move independently, allowing each high powered lens to look in a different direction. Their conical eyes have a nearly 360-degree field of view. If a threat is perceived, the chameleon may remain completely still, though they can also decide to drop to the ground. This usually doesn't cause injury and is a quick way to escape.

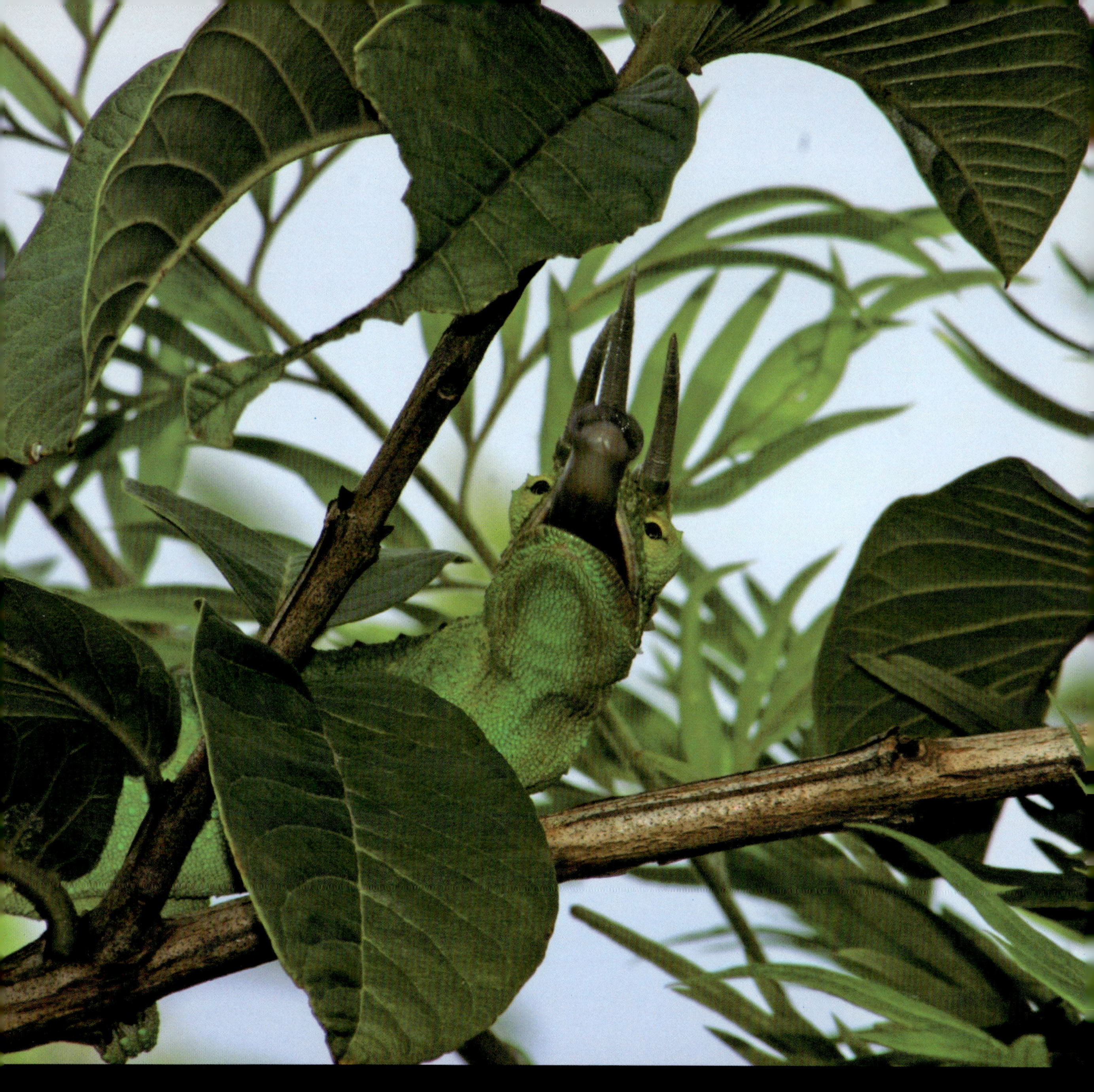

Just Before the Zap!

Both eyes are focusing on the live prey, which will become a meal in an instant

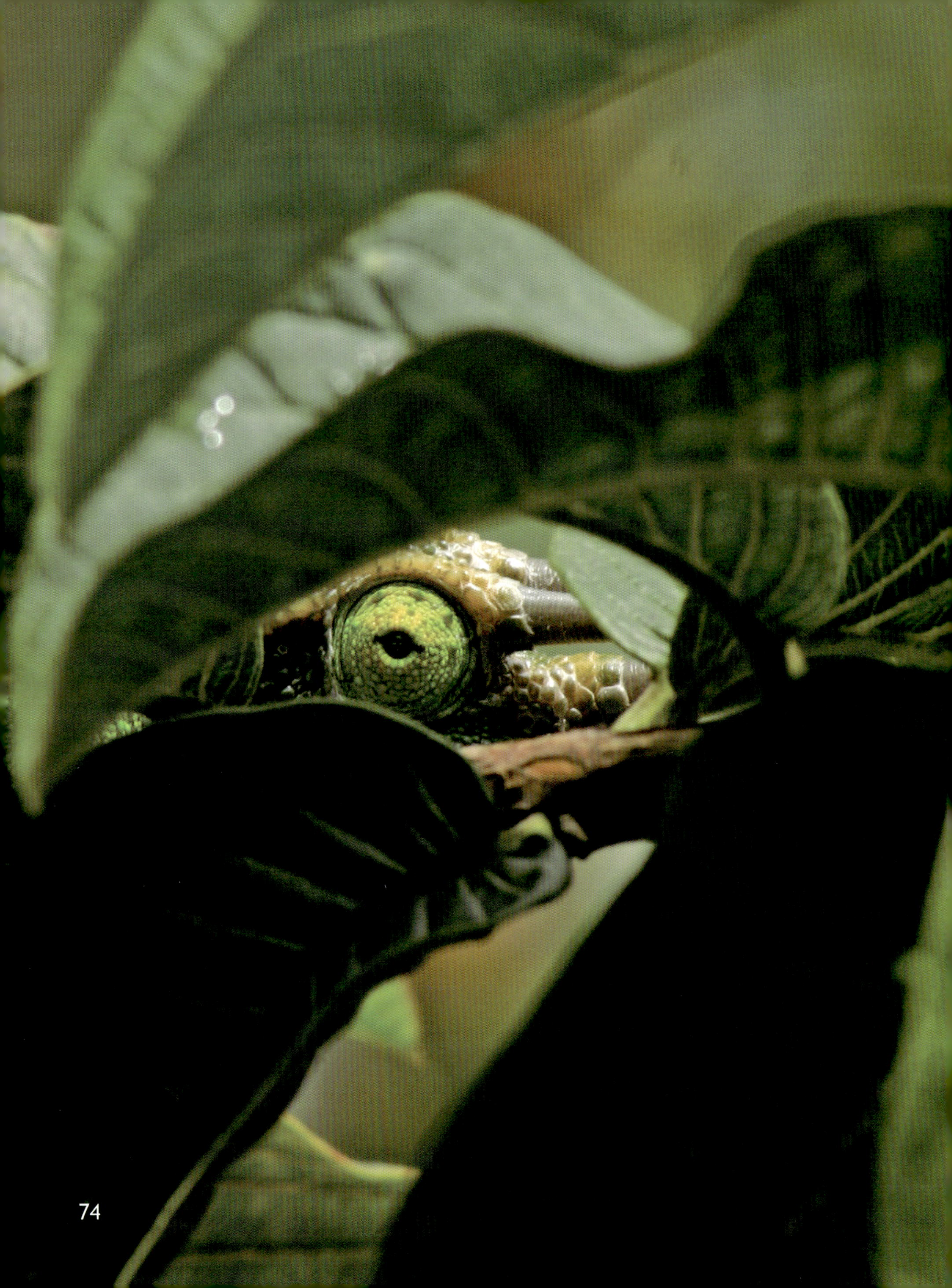

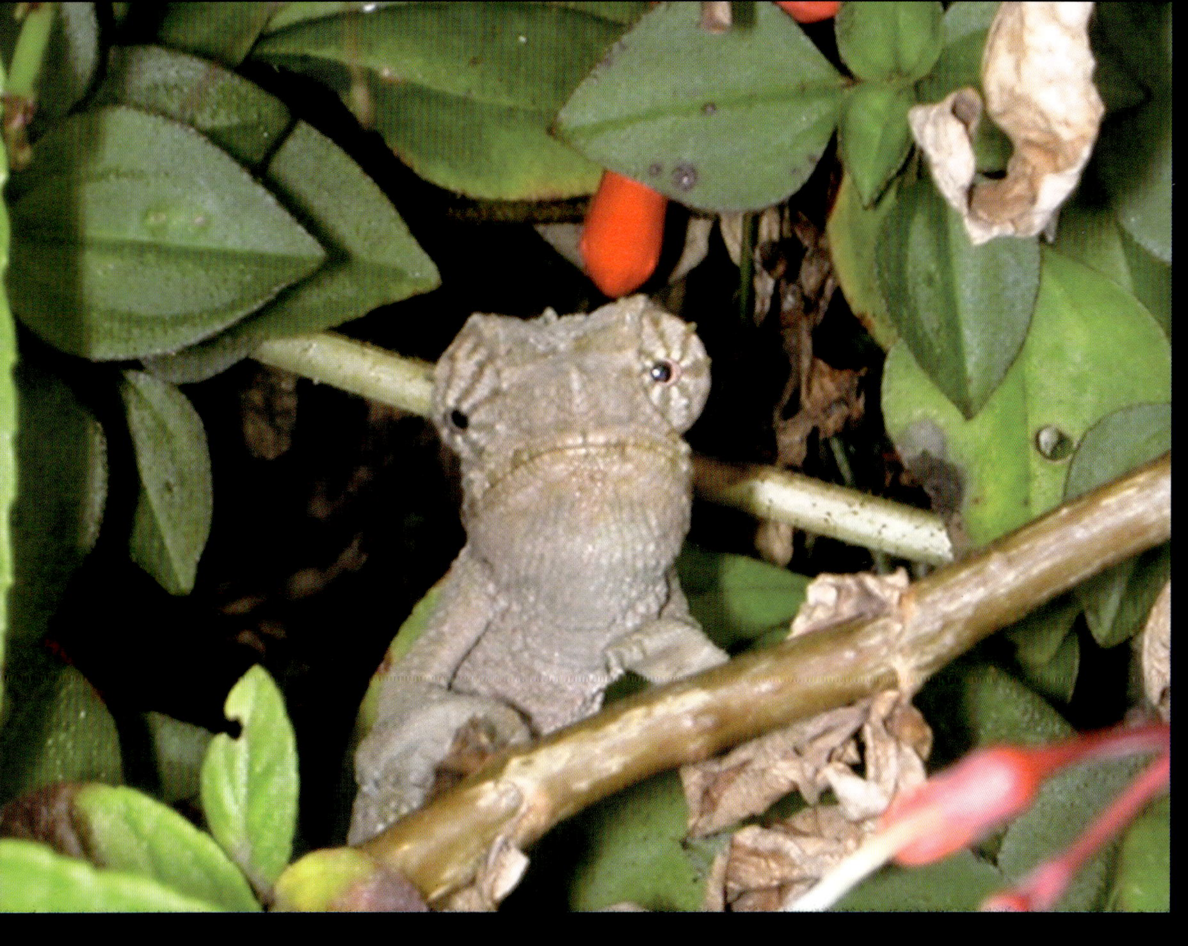

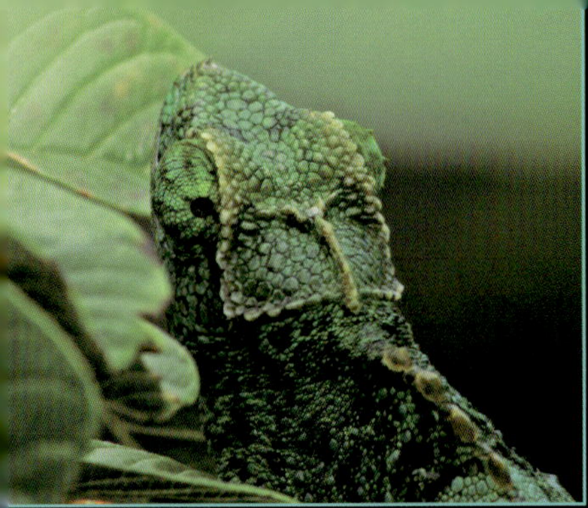

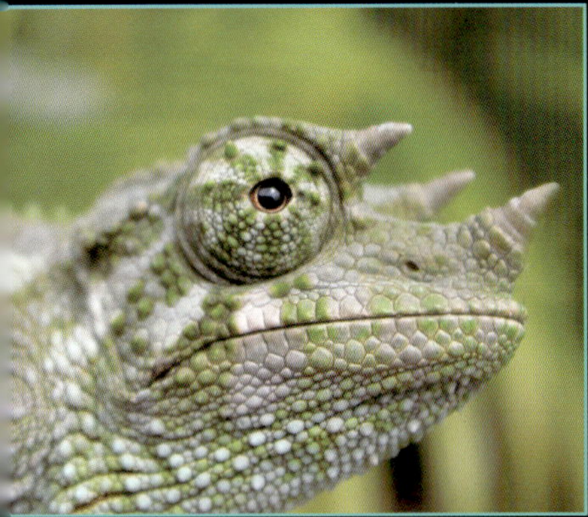

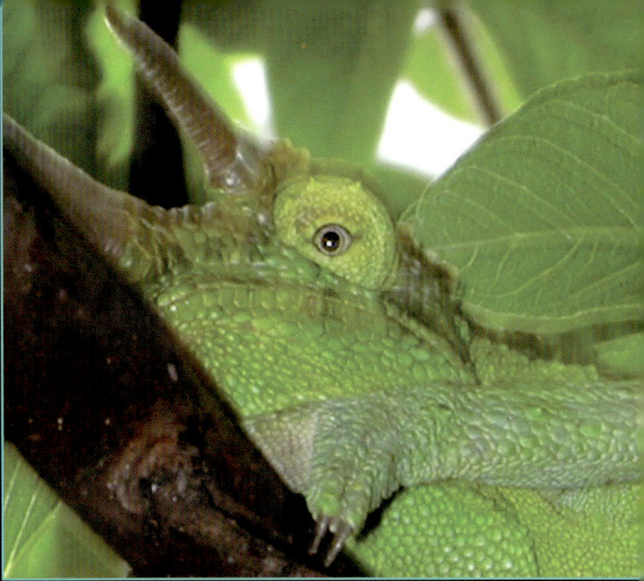

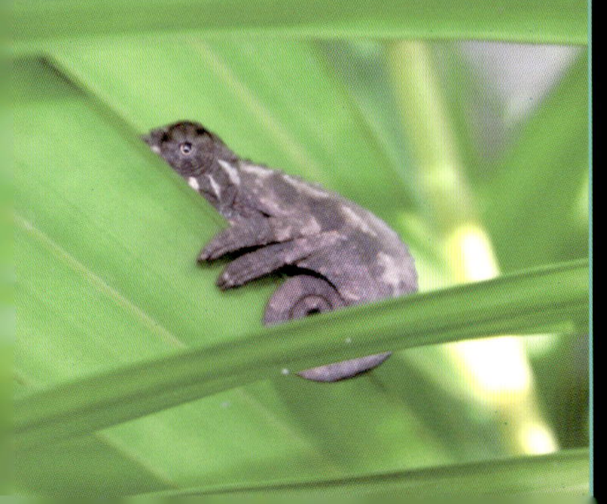
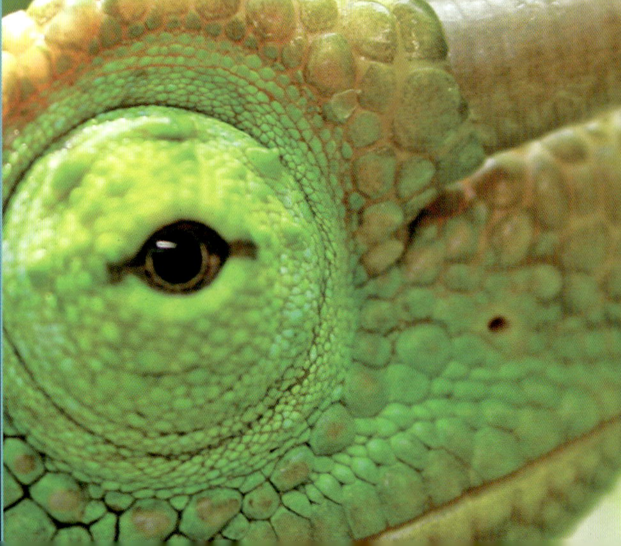

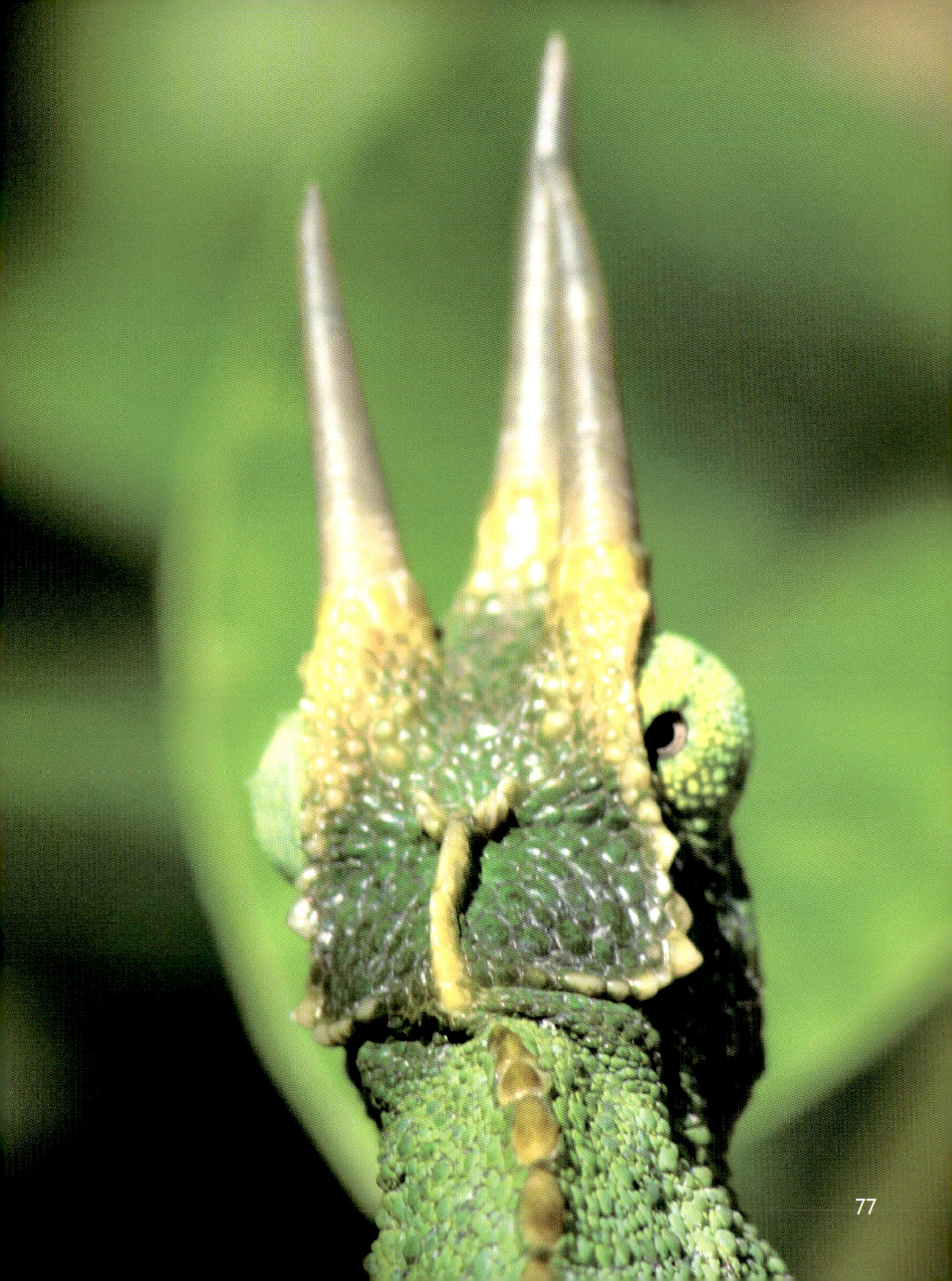

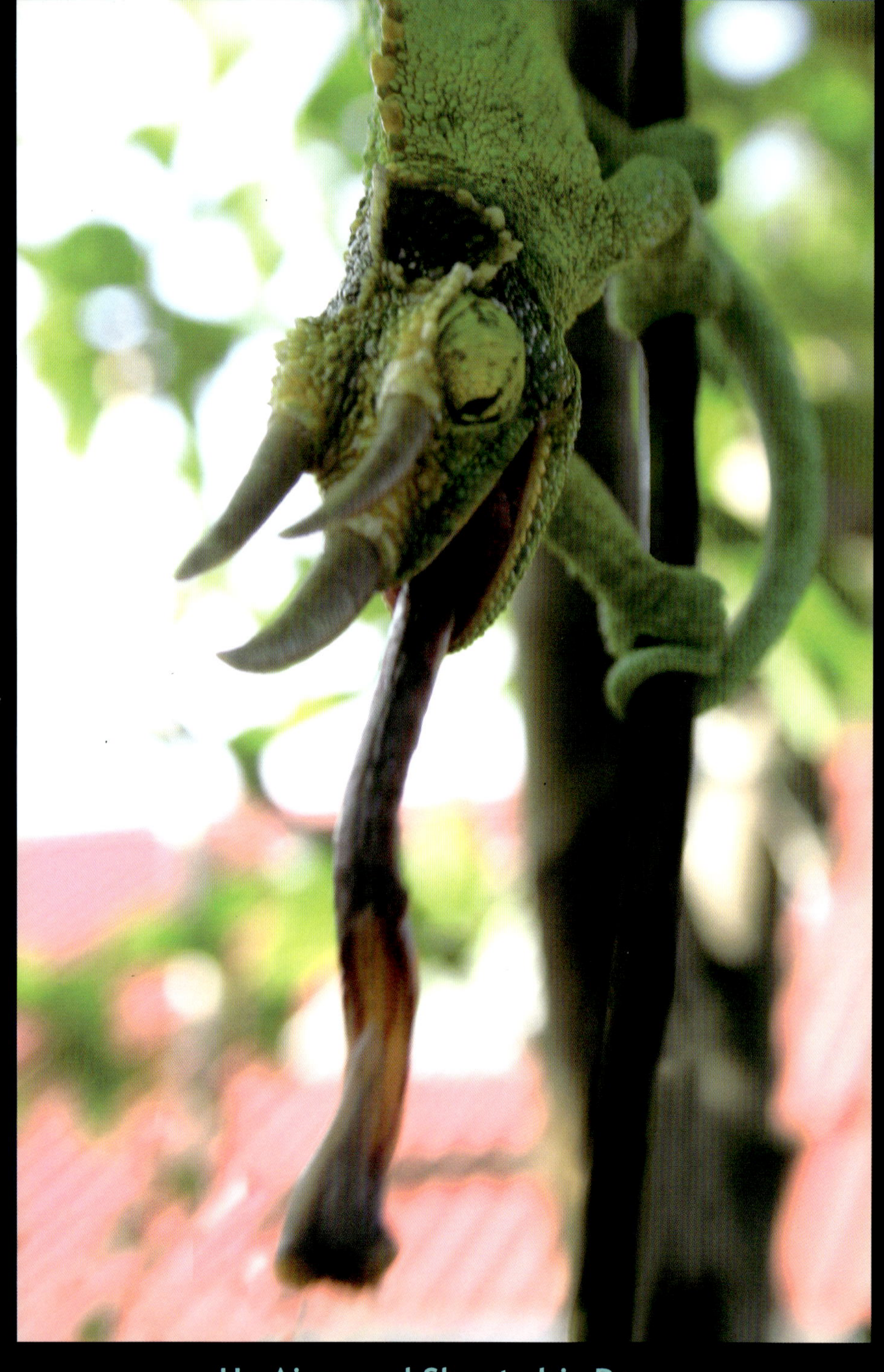

He Aims and Shoots his Prey

In less than a second, the tongue shoots, extending up to a body length and a half. It captures a live insect by gripping it with the muscular tip. An elastic-like retracting motion snaps it back into the mouth. Chewing begins!

He Didn't Go for the Honeybee

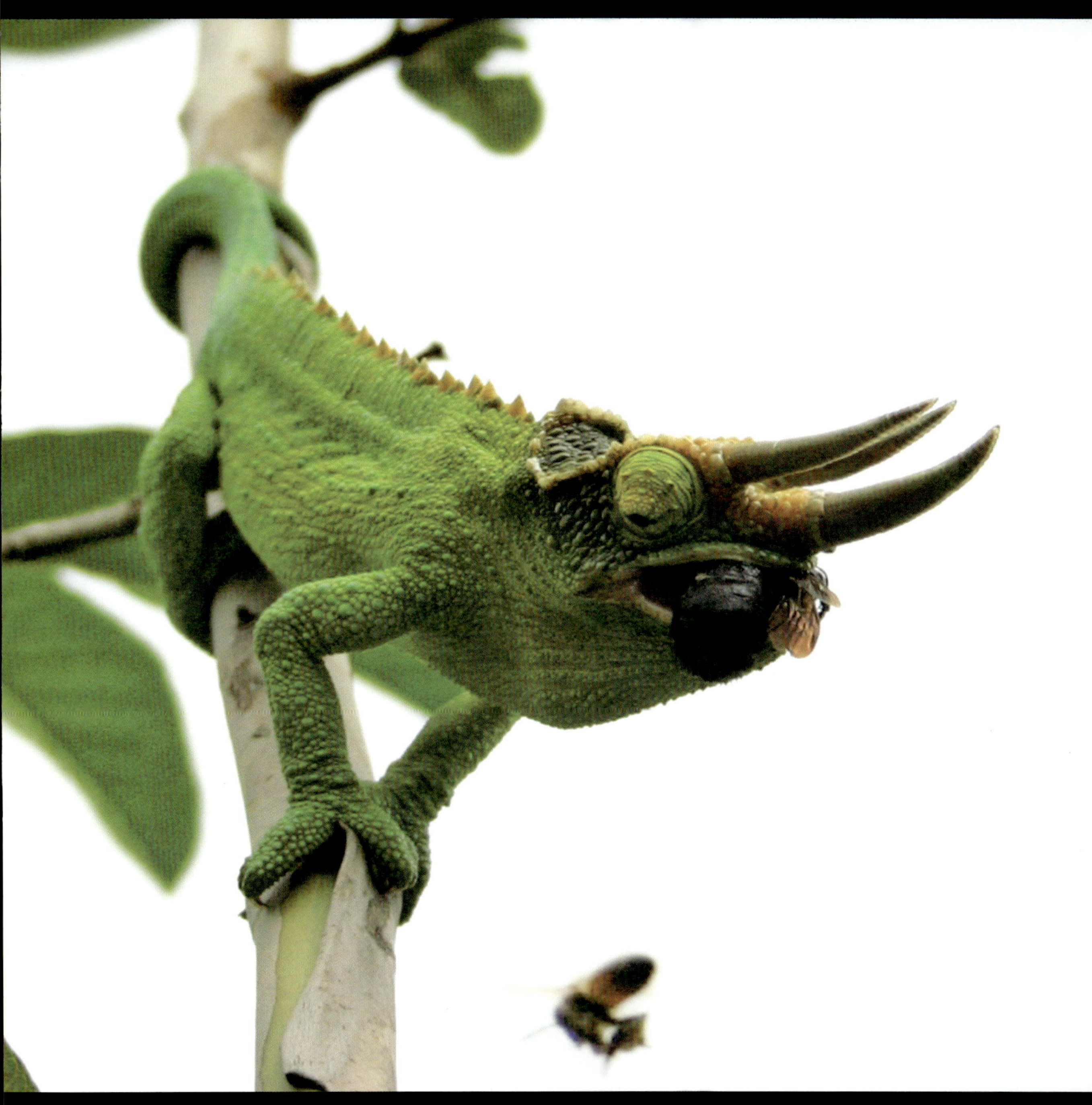

Alii Shot a Carpenter Bee Right Out of the Air

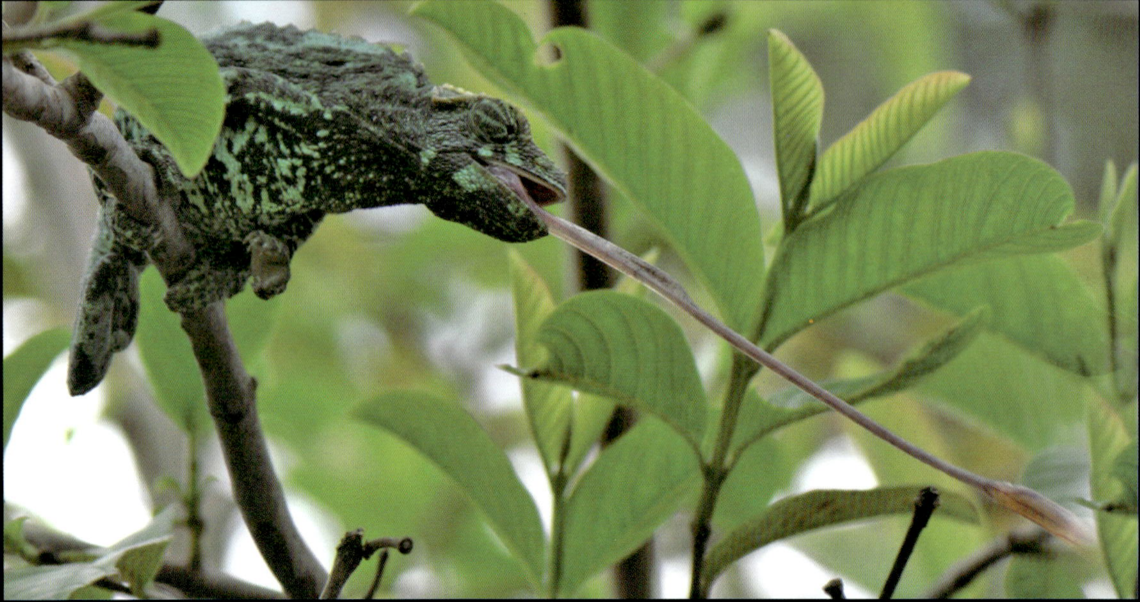

She Zaps a Bug!

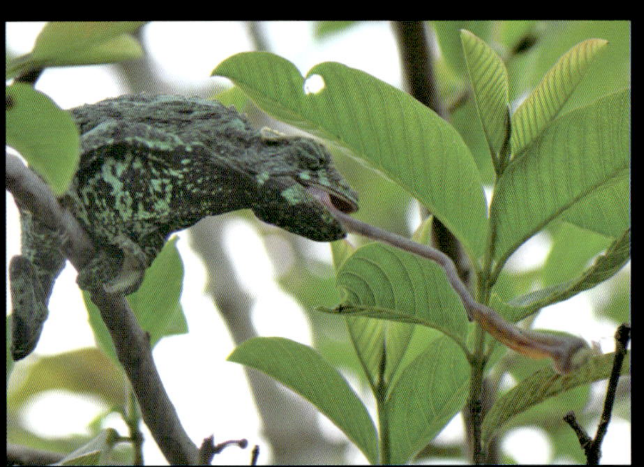

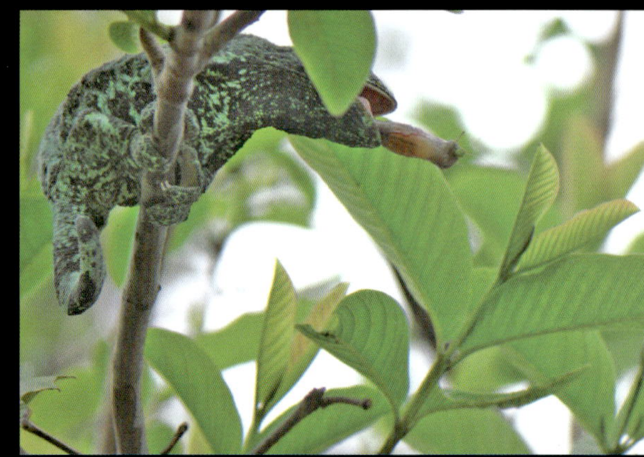

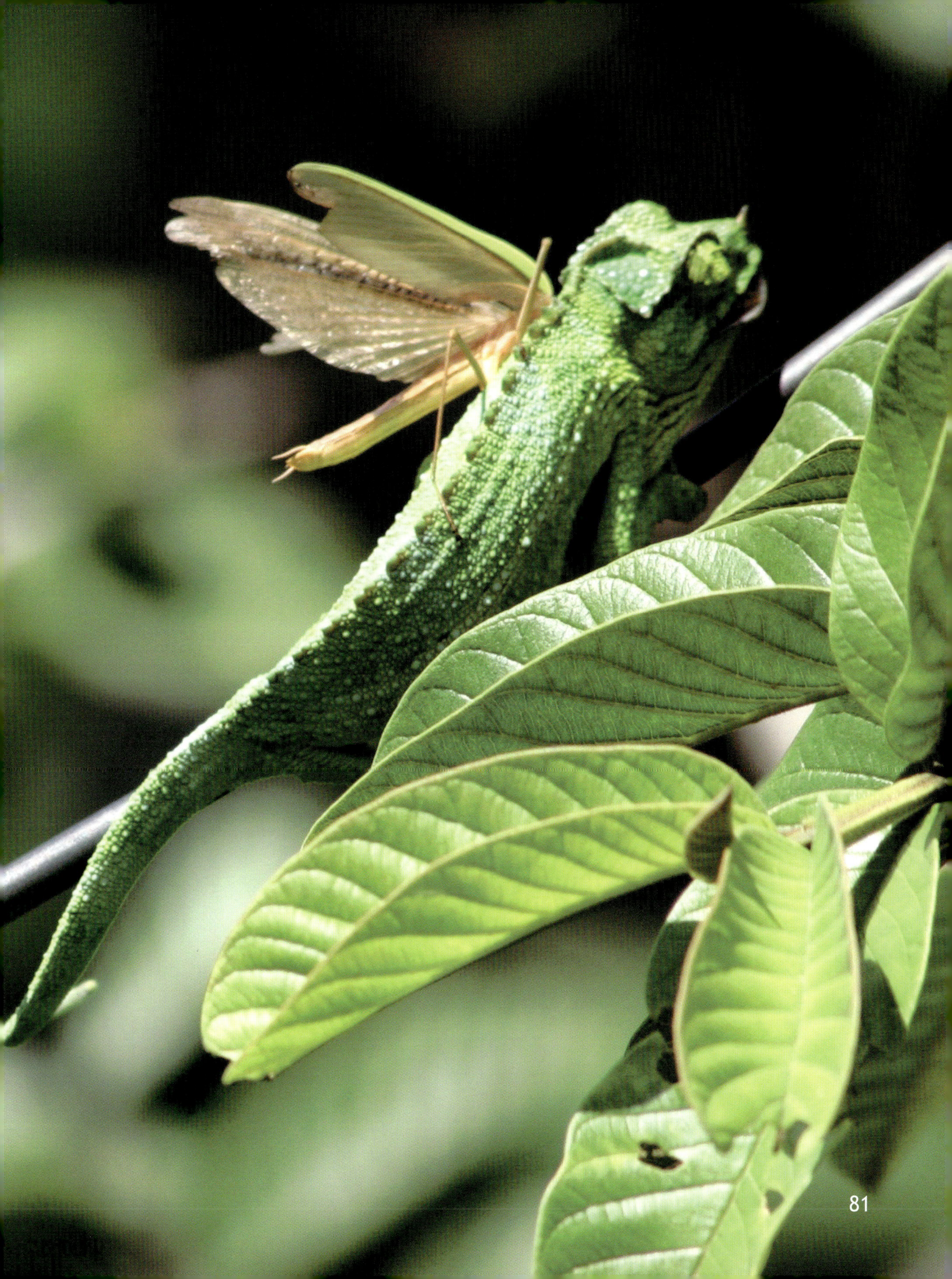

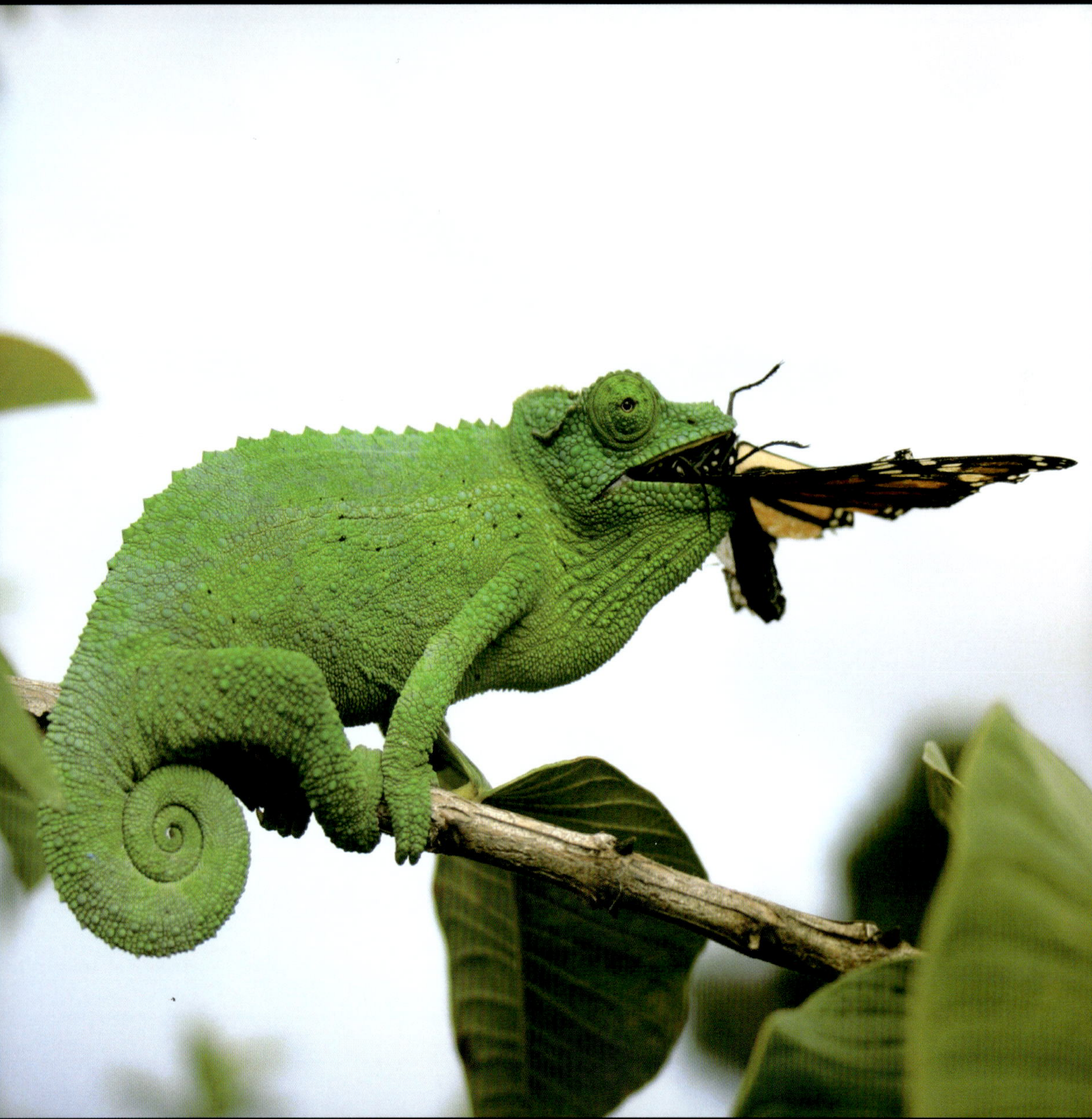

Maybe this was an opportunity that looked too tasty to pass up. Perhaps it's a matter of preference and another individual would not eat a butterfly or a bee. A wrong choice could mean a sting, a bite or a toxin that could be fatal, but in this instance it was not the case. Variety in the diet of live prey creates a nutritious menu.

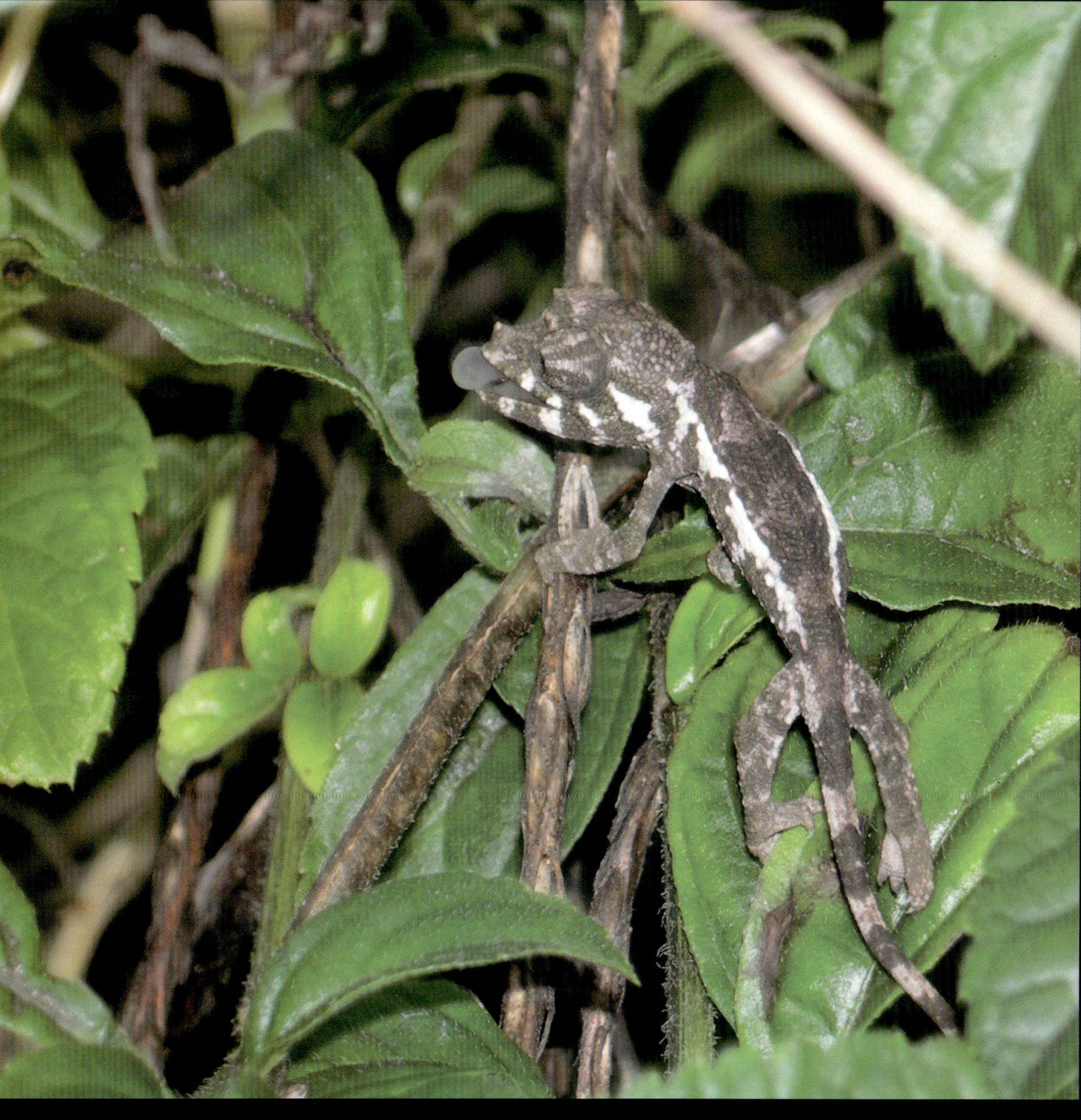

Finding food and water are priorities for neonates that begin hunting very soon after arrival. A baby is at risk for becoming a meal for a gecko, a bird or an insect such as a praying mantis. Ants can also be deadly. Even an adult chameleon could be a predator. This healthy youngster is a survivor, aggressively shooting fruit flies, which is perfect target practice for a growing boy.

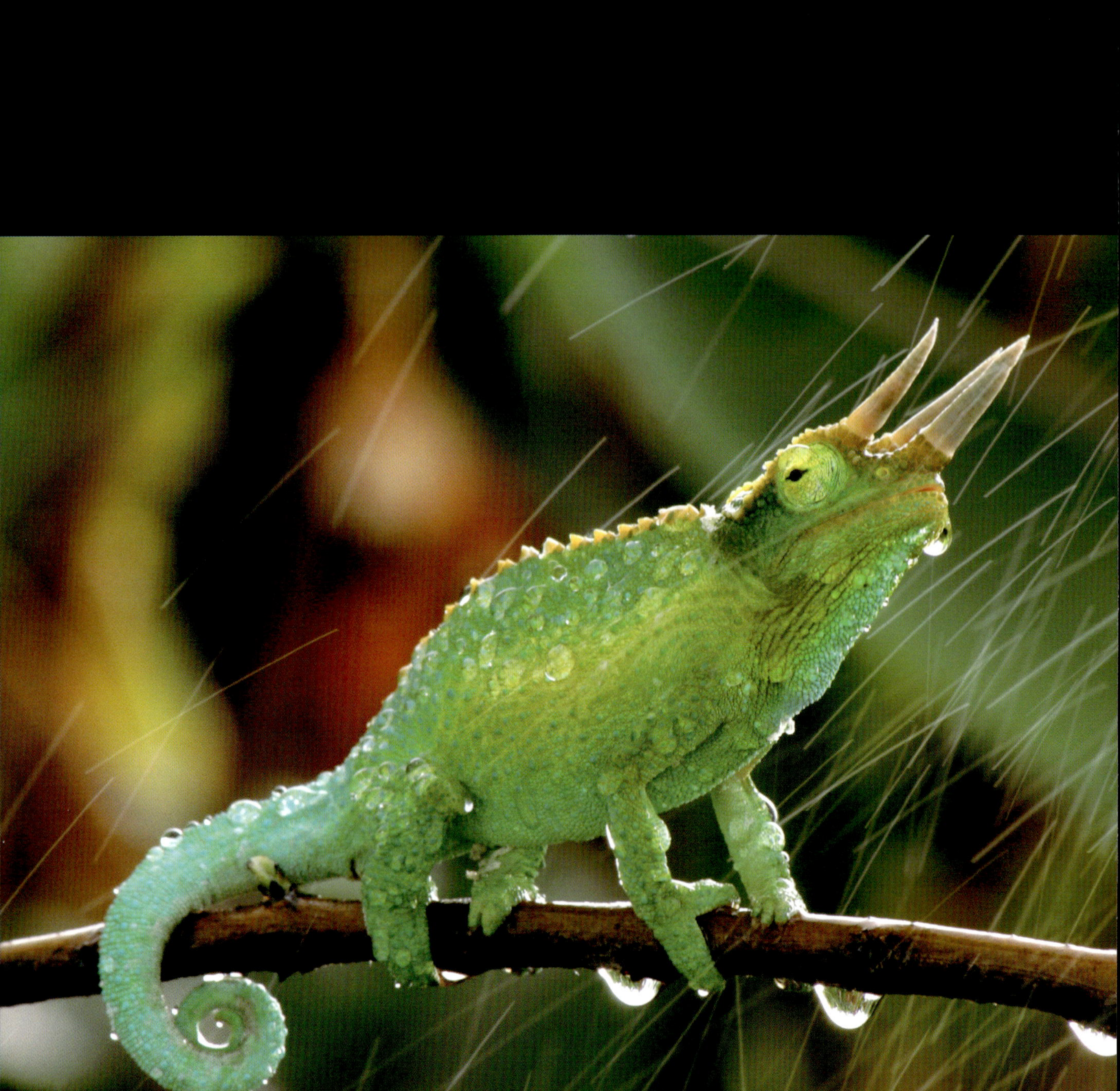

Hot Tin Roof to the Misting System

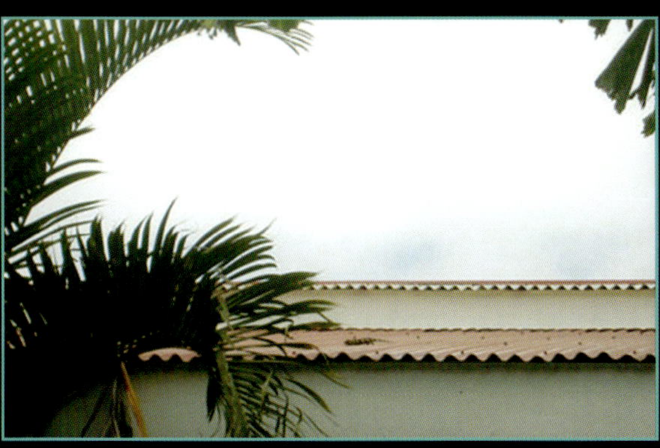

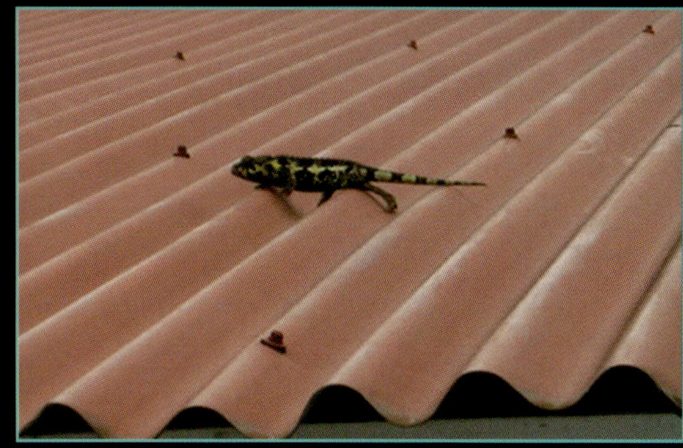

H2O Game Plan

For a chameleon, drinking is more
important than eating.

Chameleons have various strategies for taking in water. When it begins to rain, instinct may initially cause them to take cover. Once they realize it's not a threat, their lips start smacking.

Another technique involves an upside down position, allowing water to trickle on the nose or horns, making its way into the mouth.

Sometimes they can be seen tilting their heads to the side, letting raindrops from branches or leaves roll into their mouths.

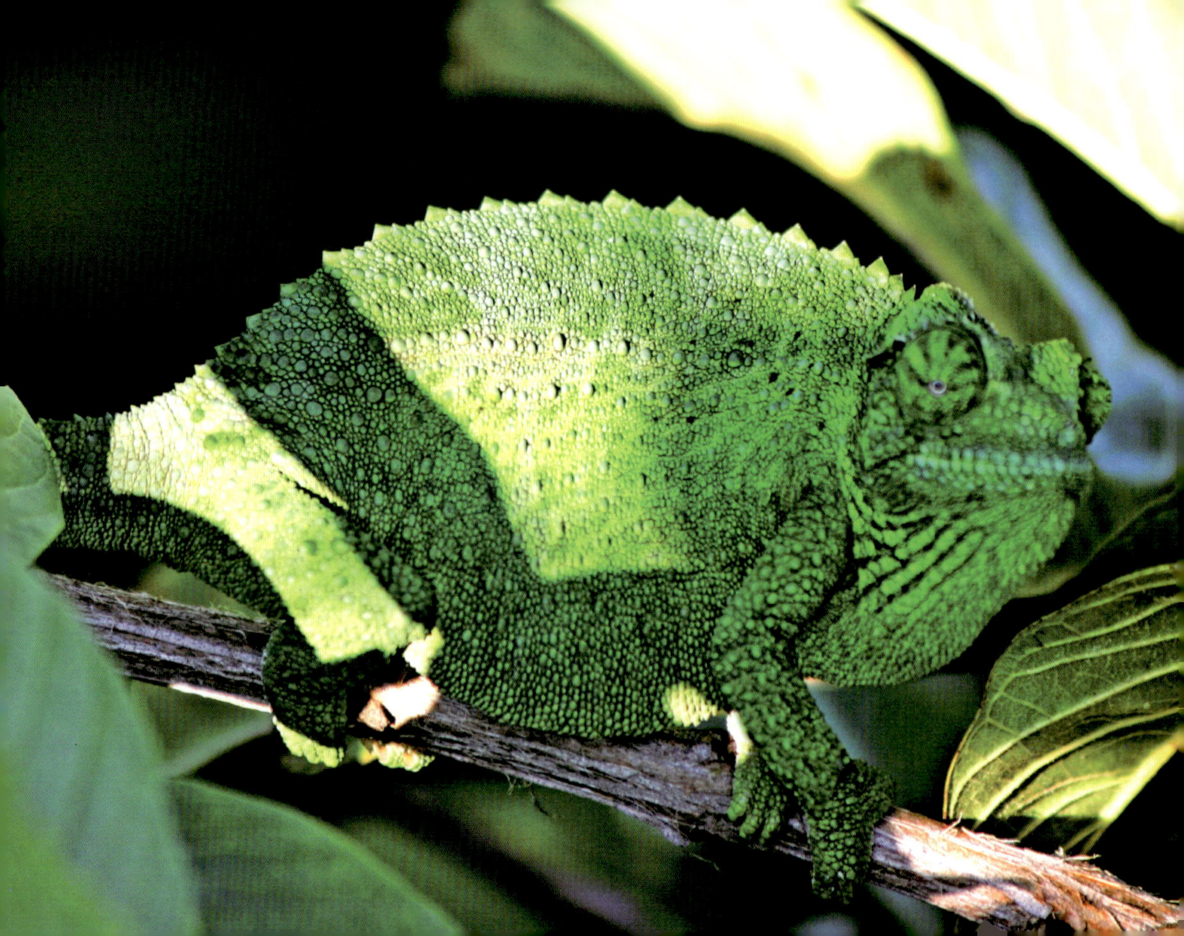

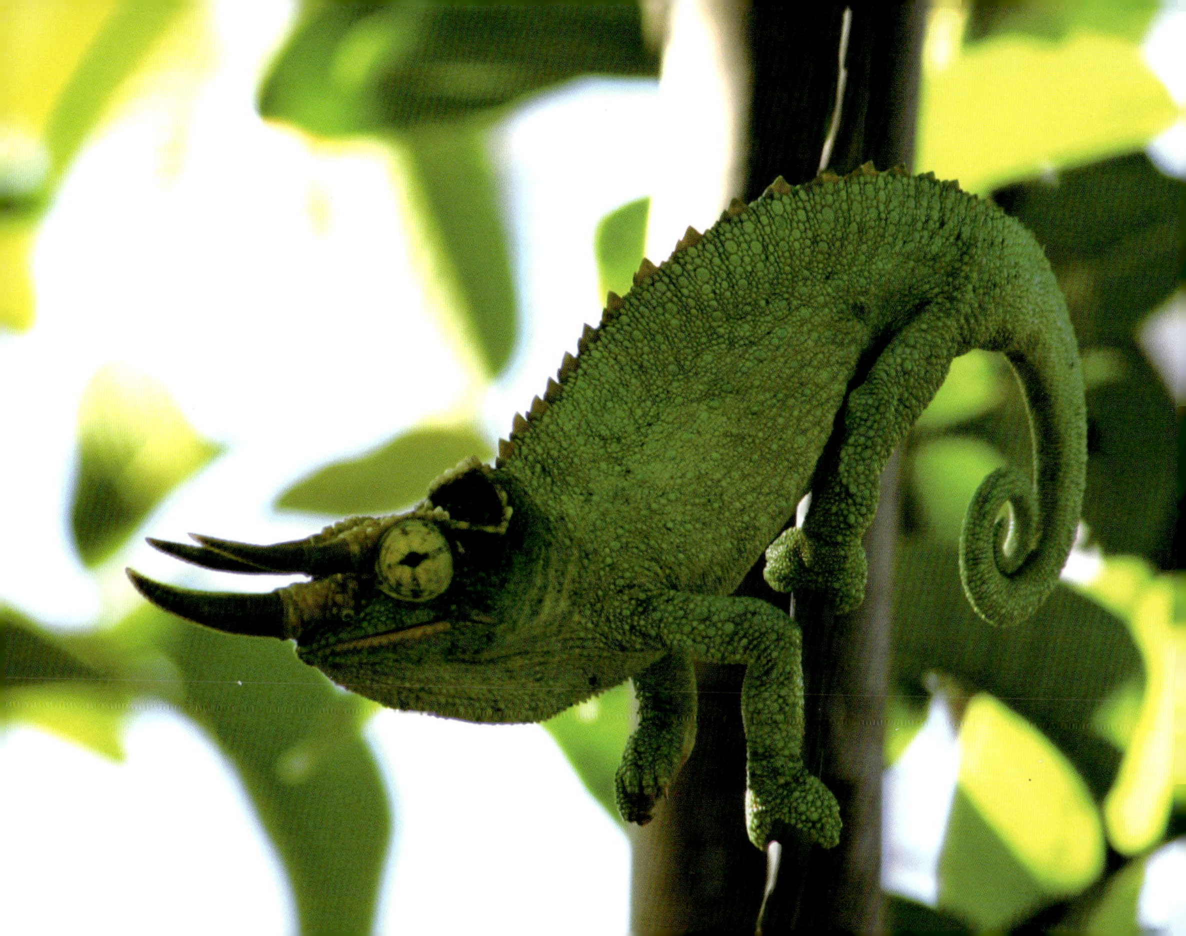

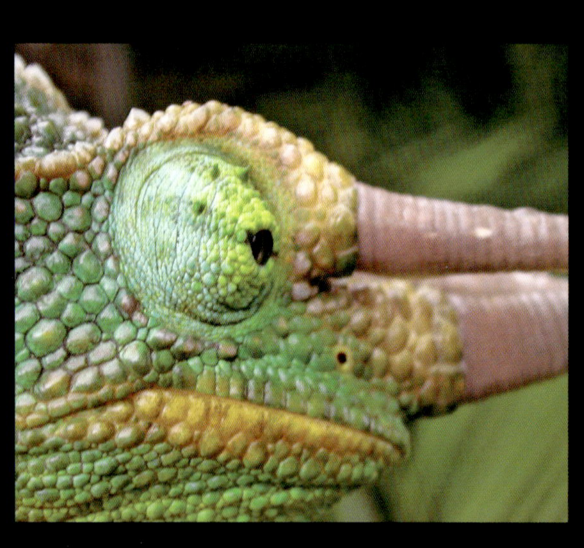

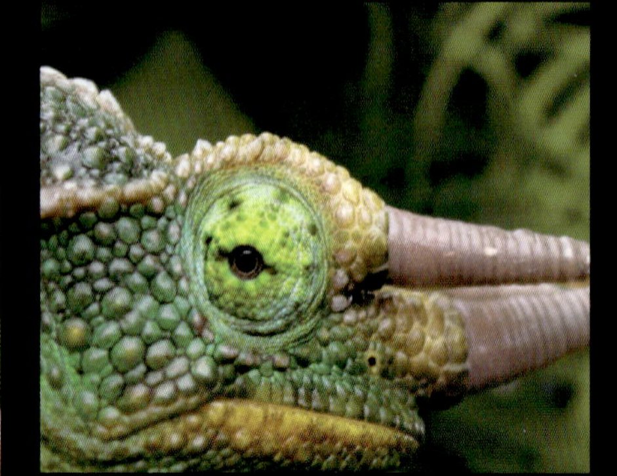

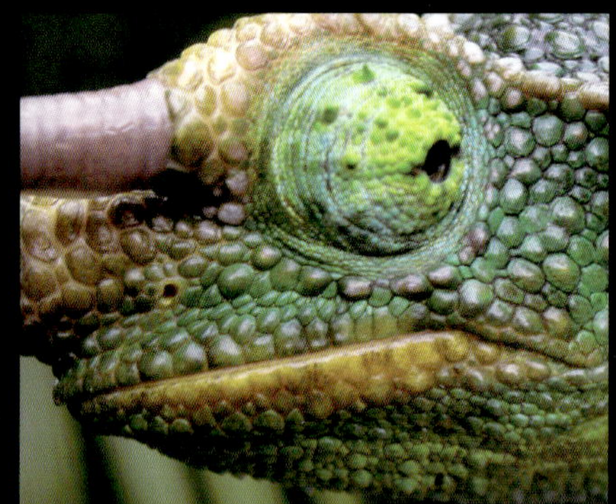

Age One Year

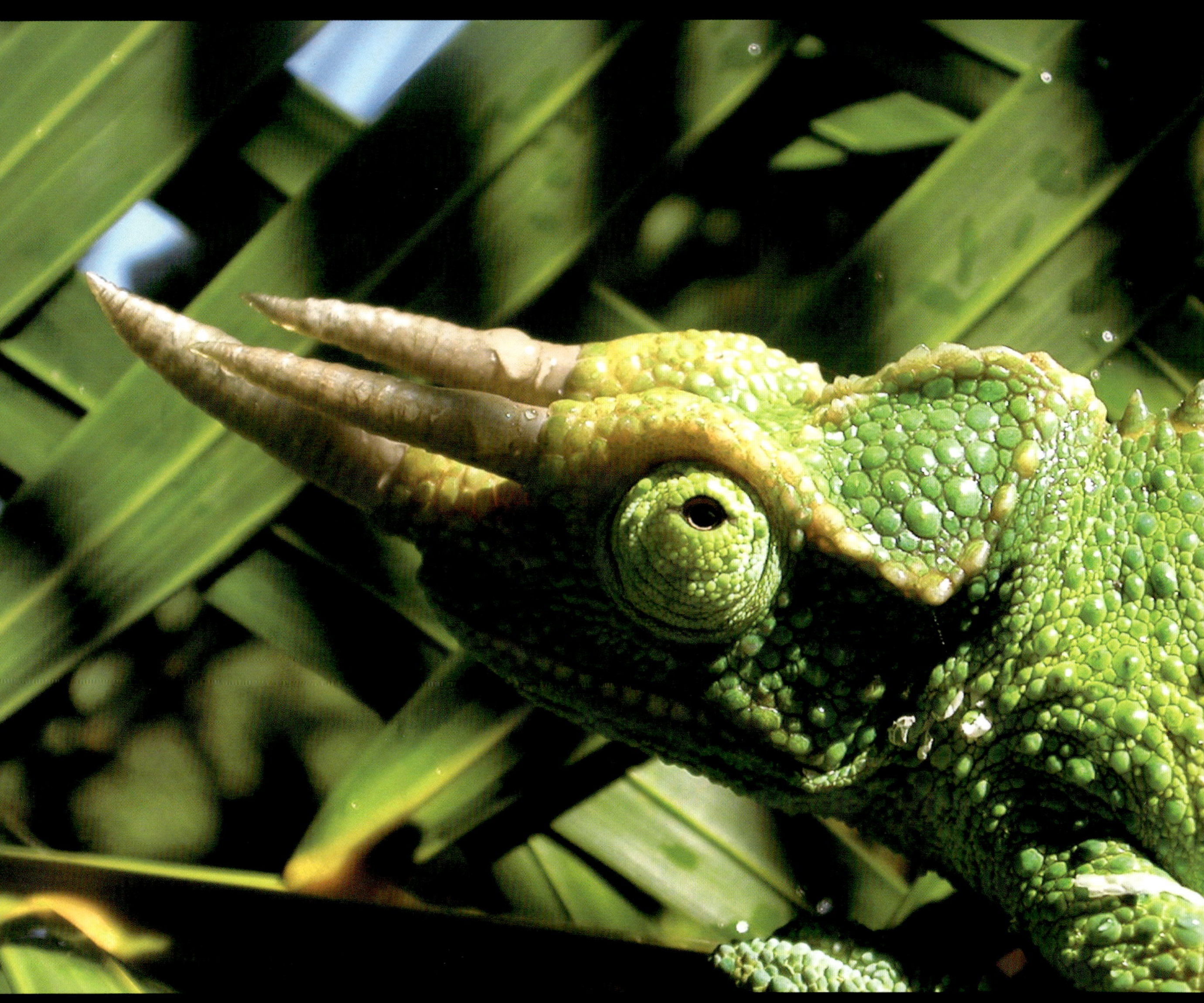

Mu, Offspring of Longhorns

Just Passing Through

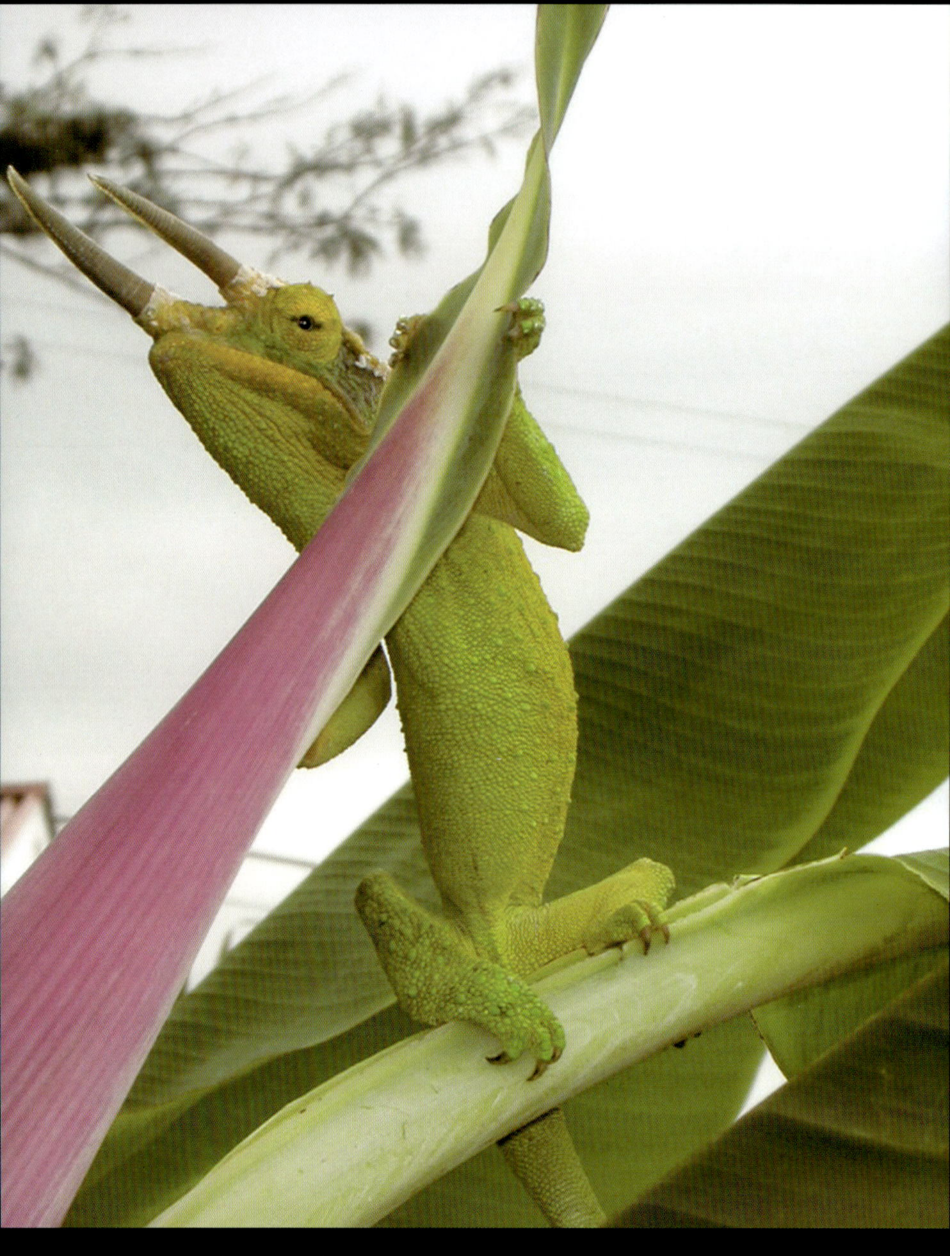

Seen only one time on the ornamental banana plant,
his bright yellow color
inspired the name, Sir Le Mone.

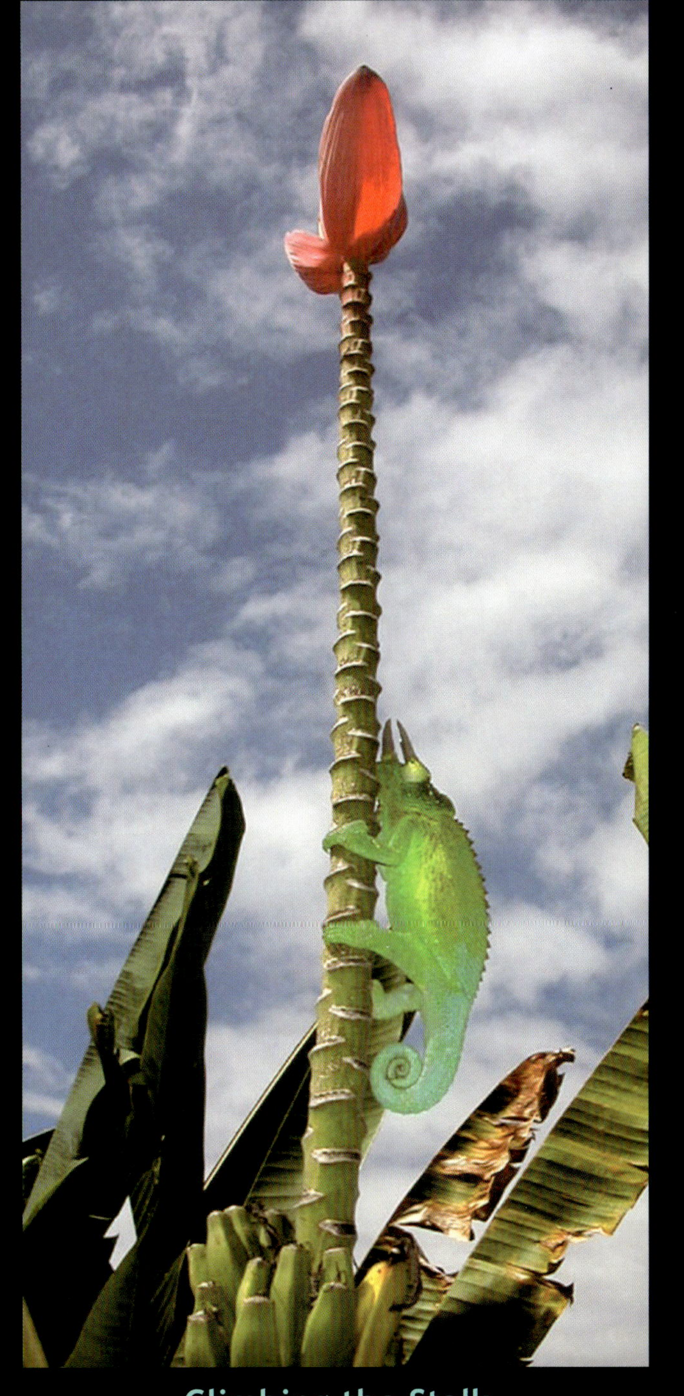

Climbing the Stalk

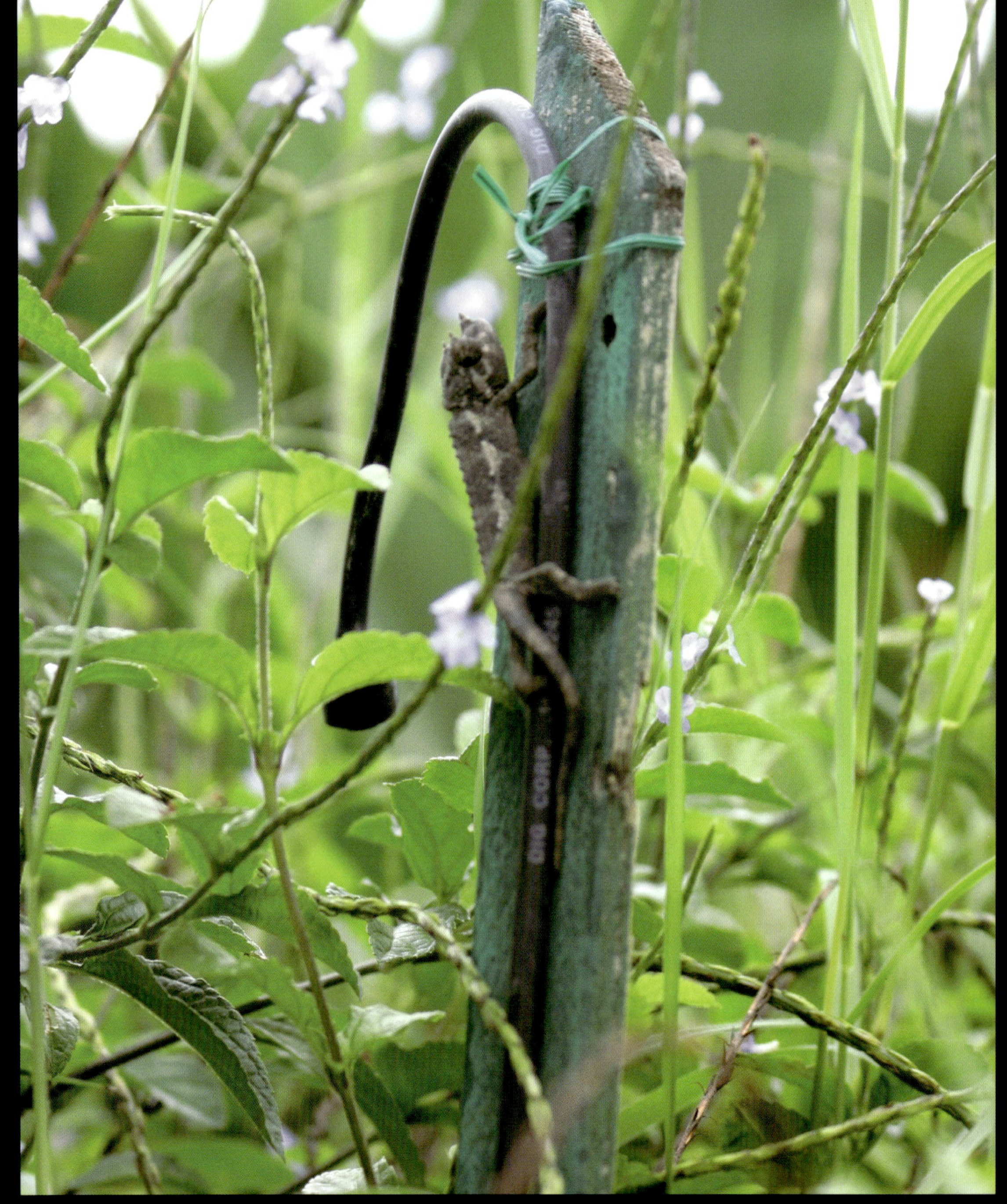

Pan Claimed the Green Stick Territory

From the time he was a juvenile, Pan could be seen on or around the green stick that supports the misting tube. This is a chameleon's prime real estate, as it is a water source. There is also a great view of the females as well as approaching rivals.

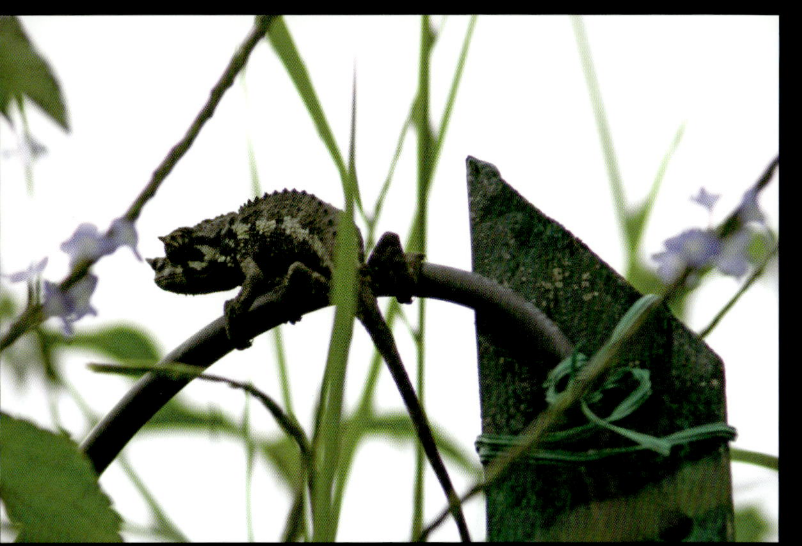

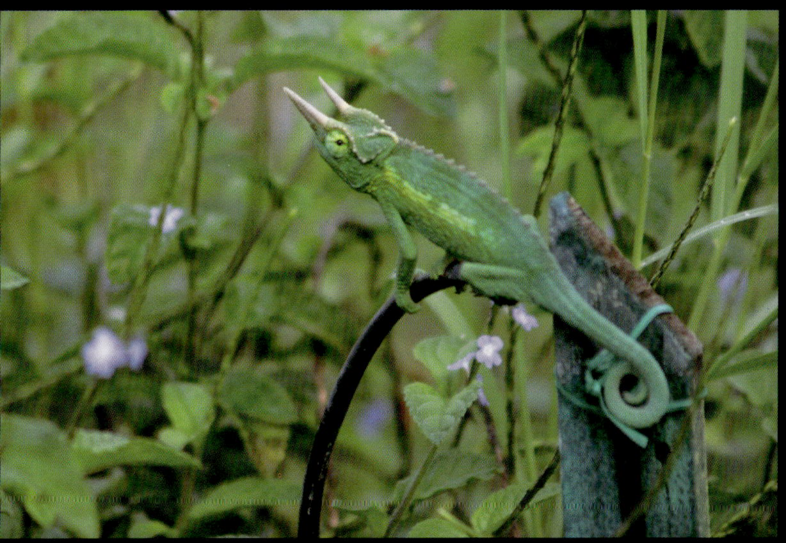

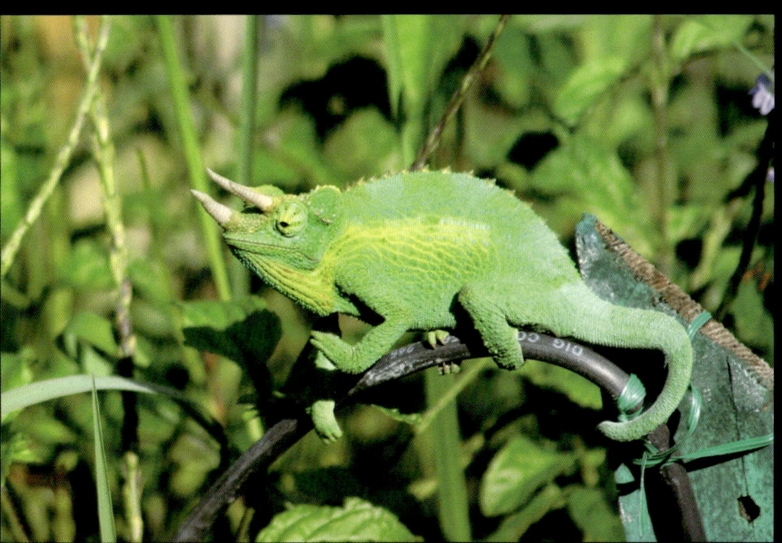

Portraits of Pan

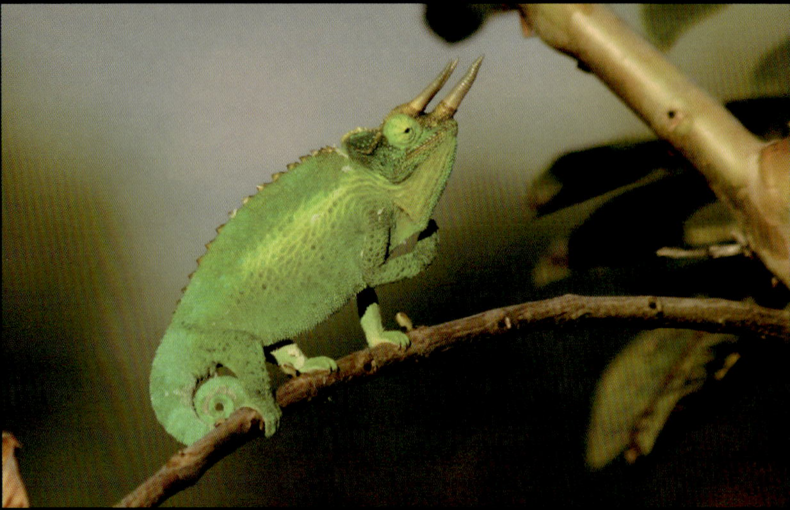

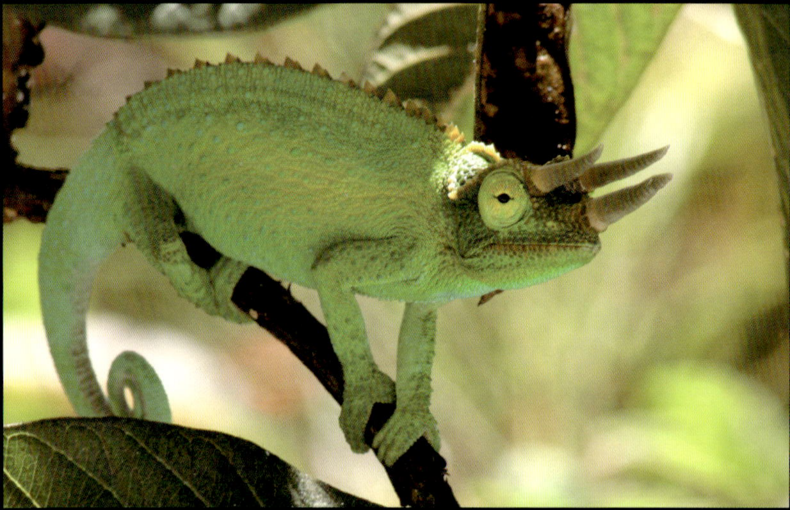

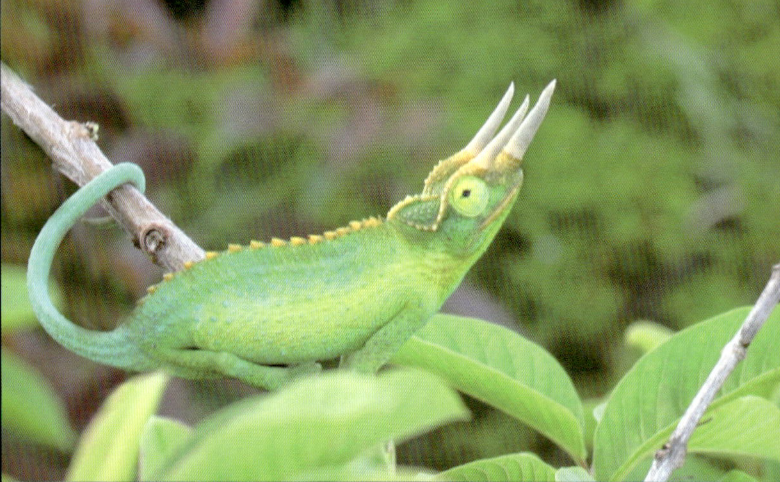

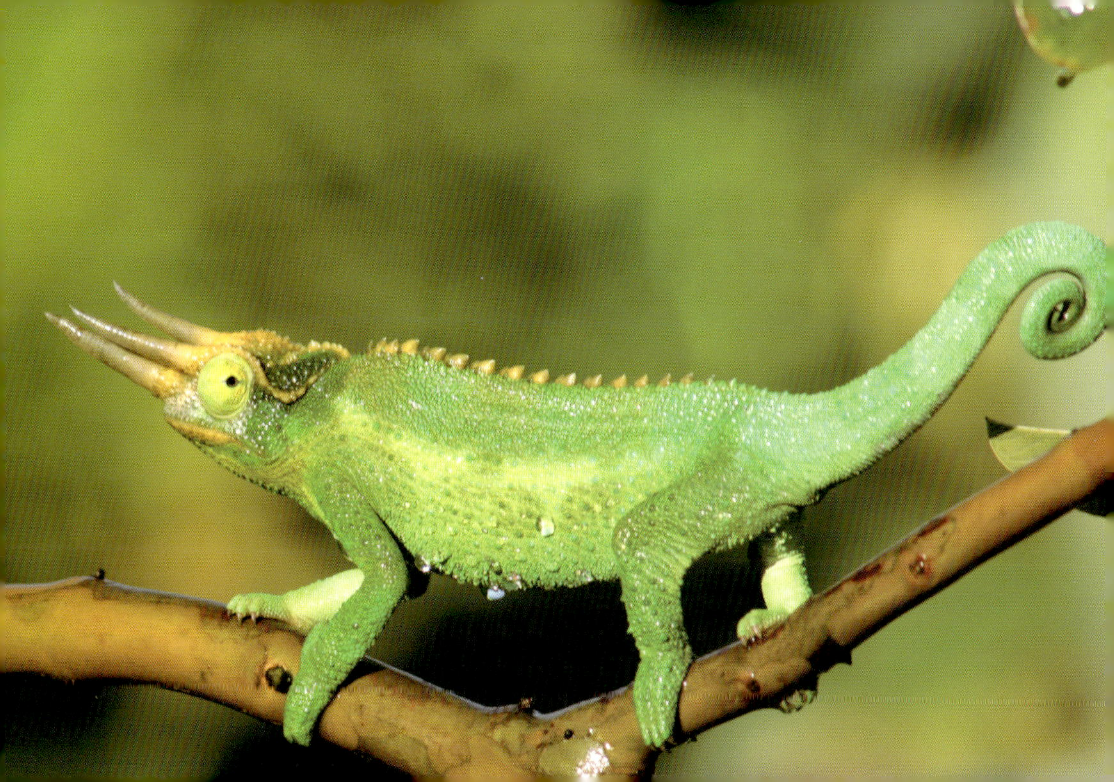

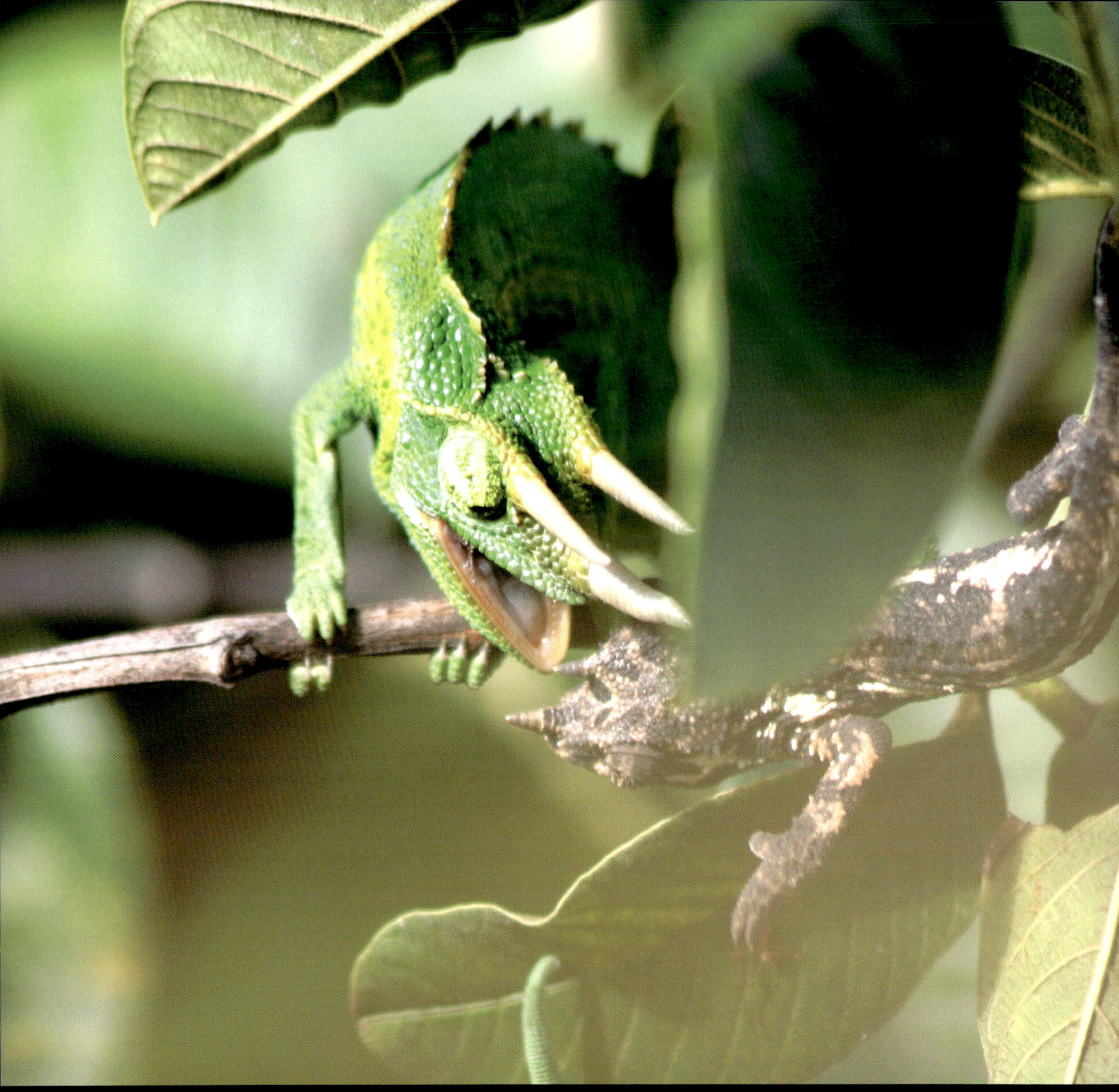

Pan Guards his Territory

The alpha male will tolerate baby or juvenile males
in his territory,
but when they reach sub-adulthood
they are considered rivals.

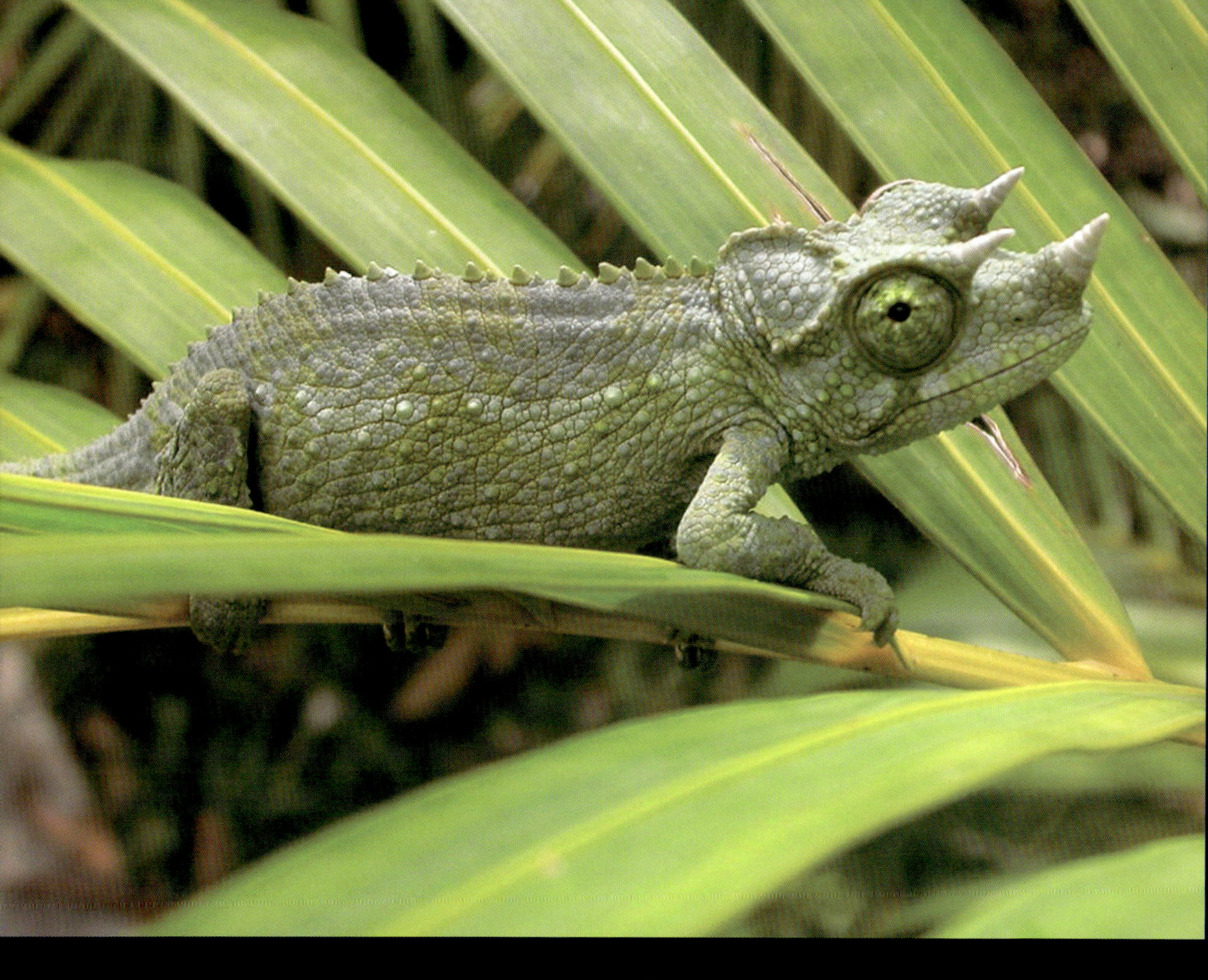

Chamelot

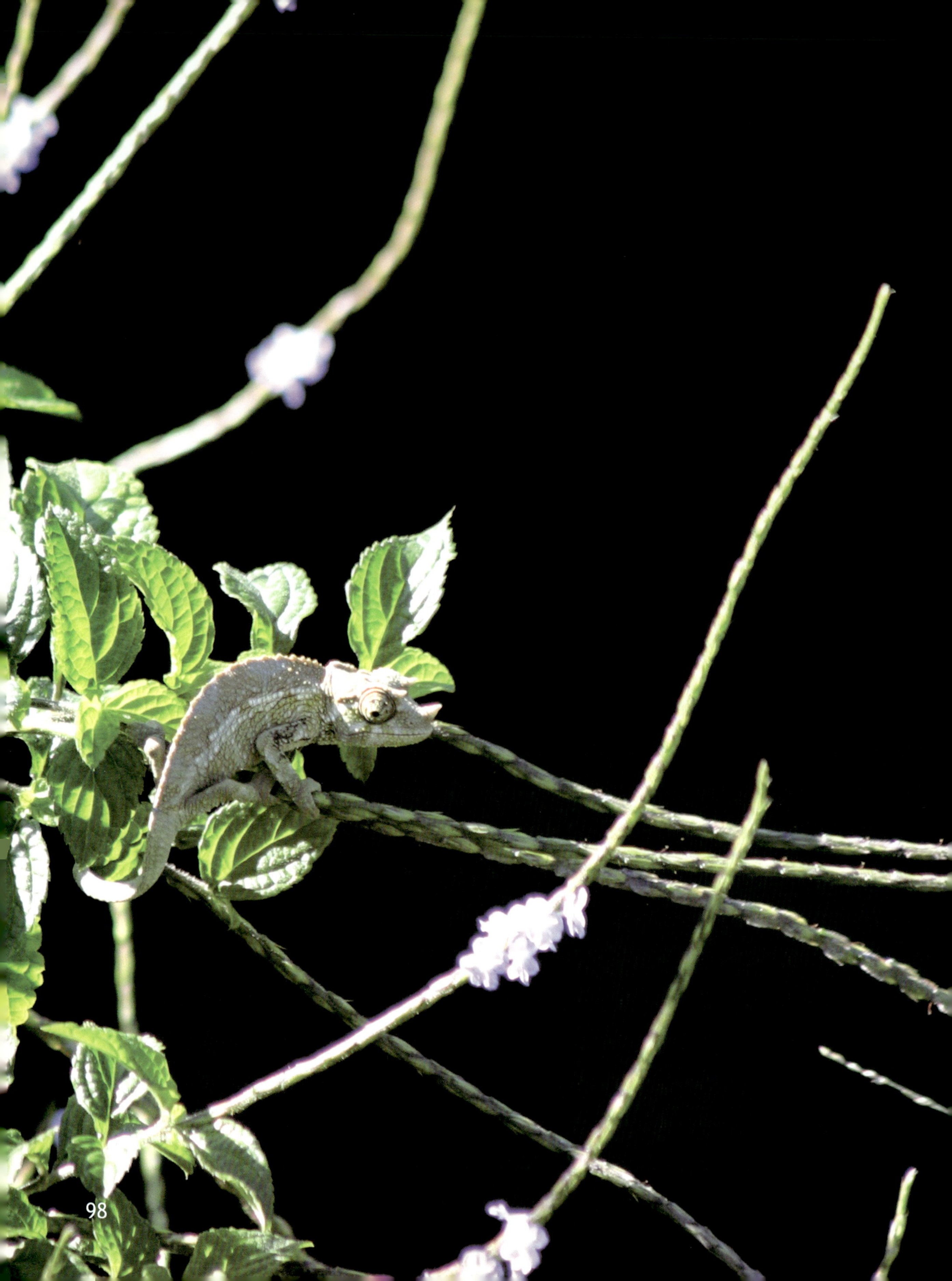

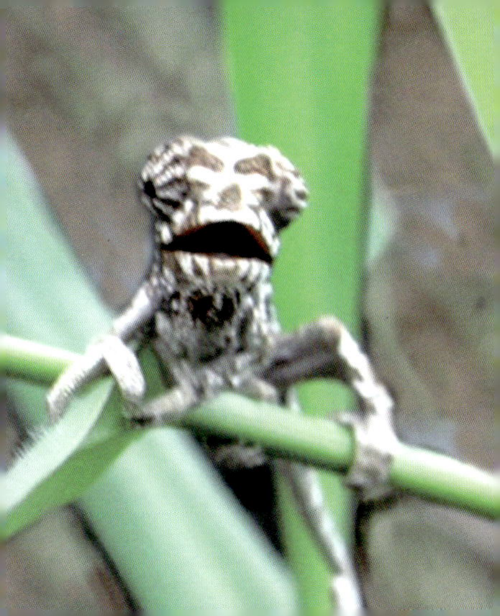

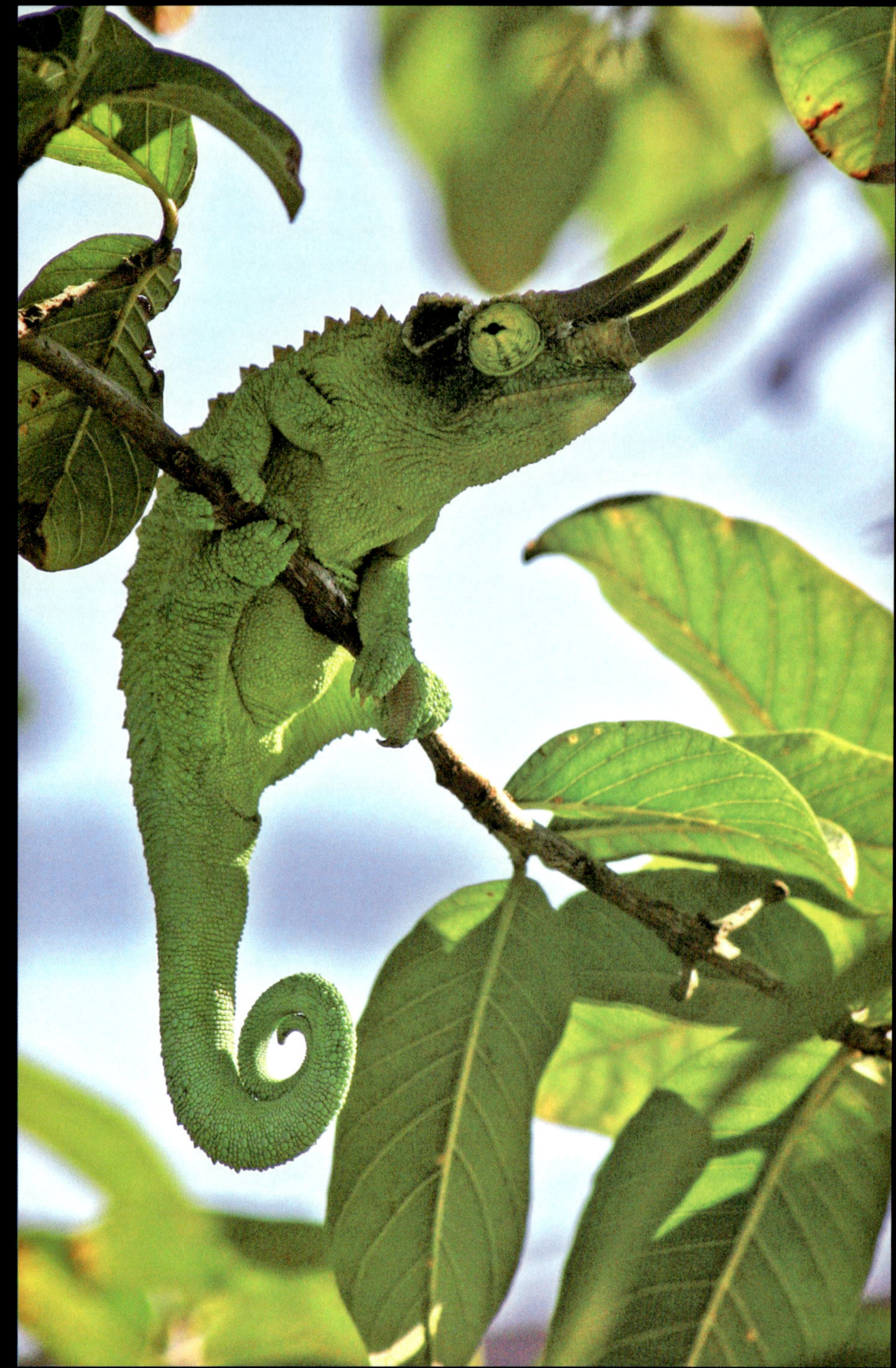

Tarzan

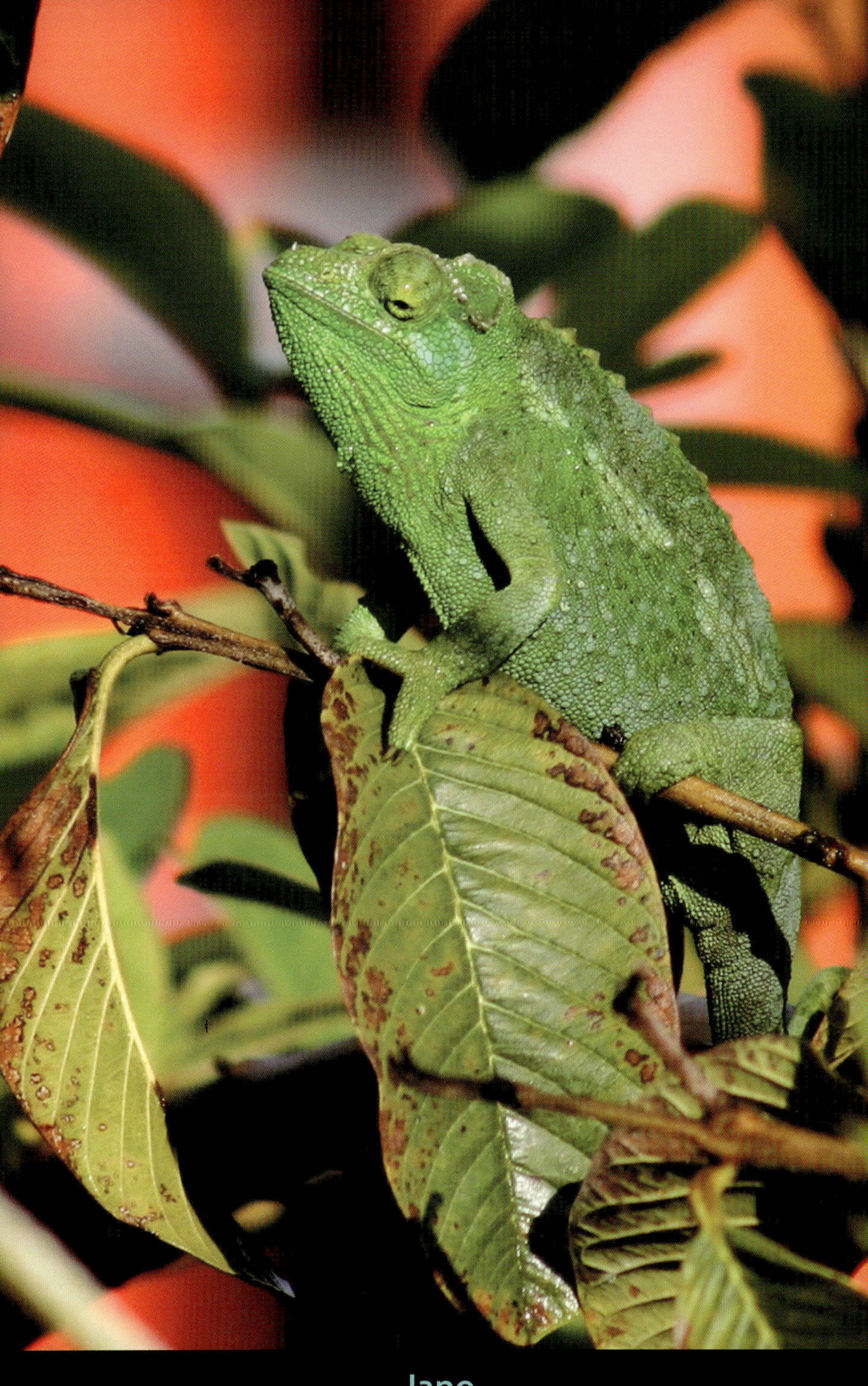

Jane

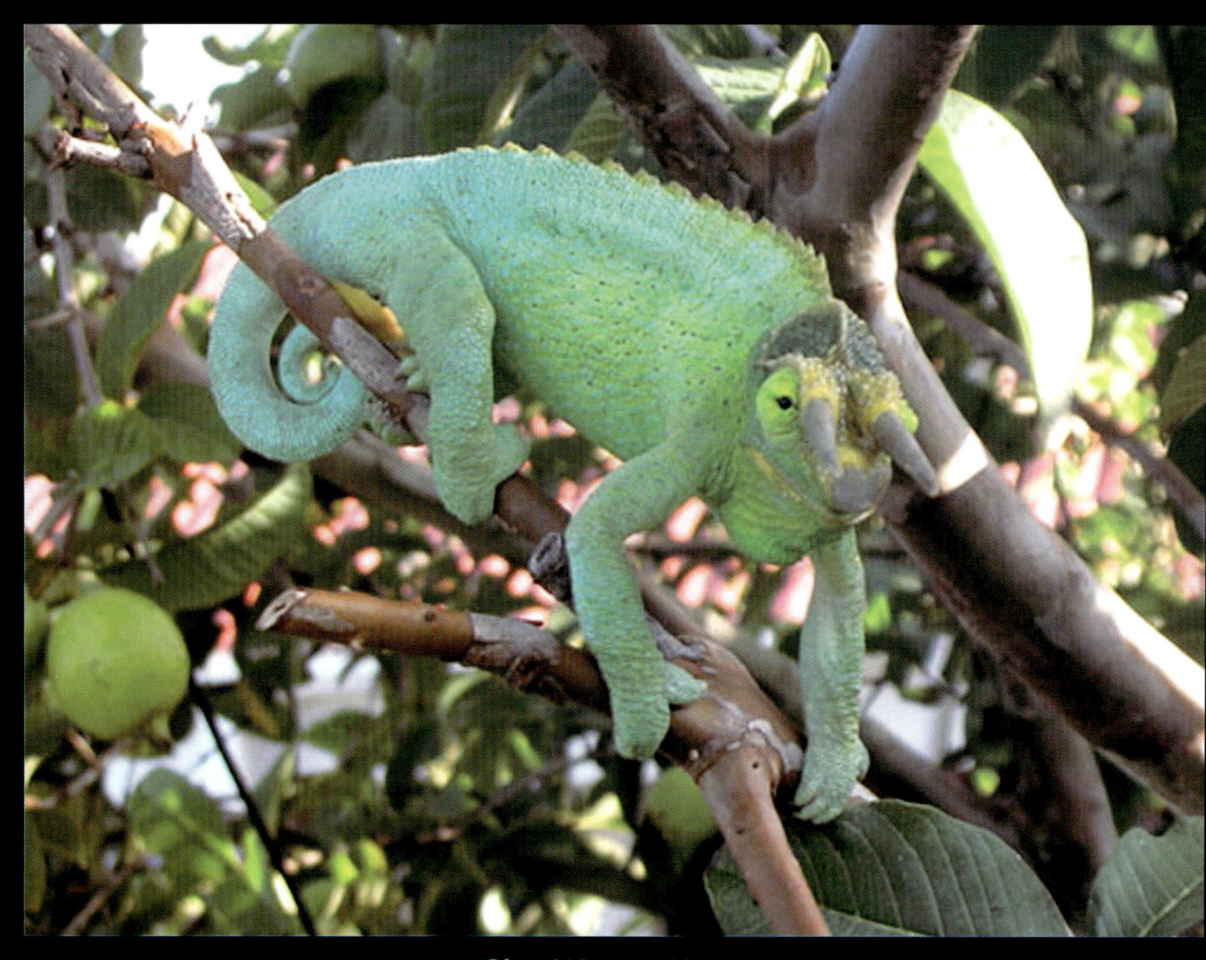

She Wants Me

Spunk Bob and Guava Gal

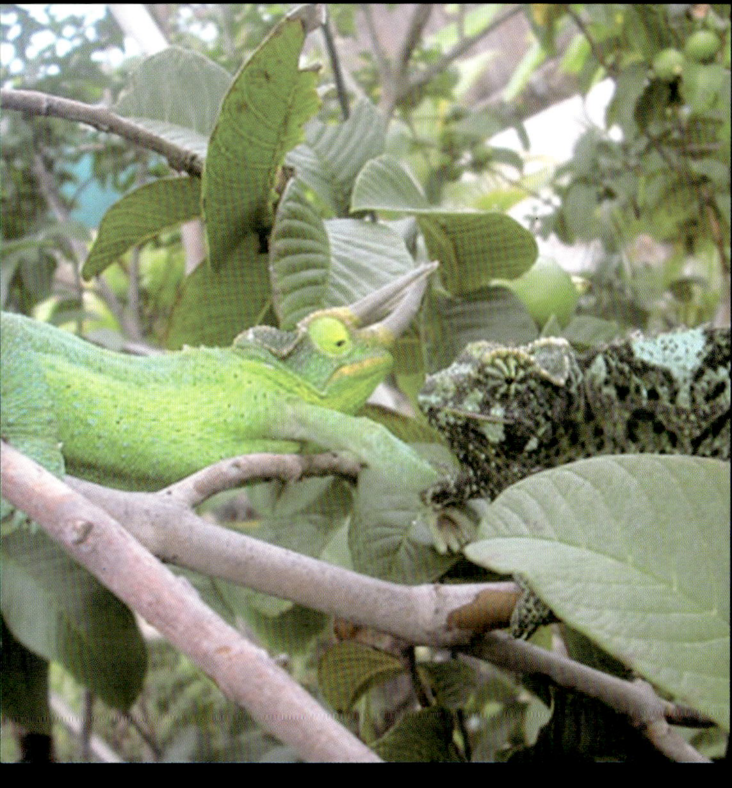

I Just Wanna Hold Your Hand

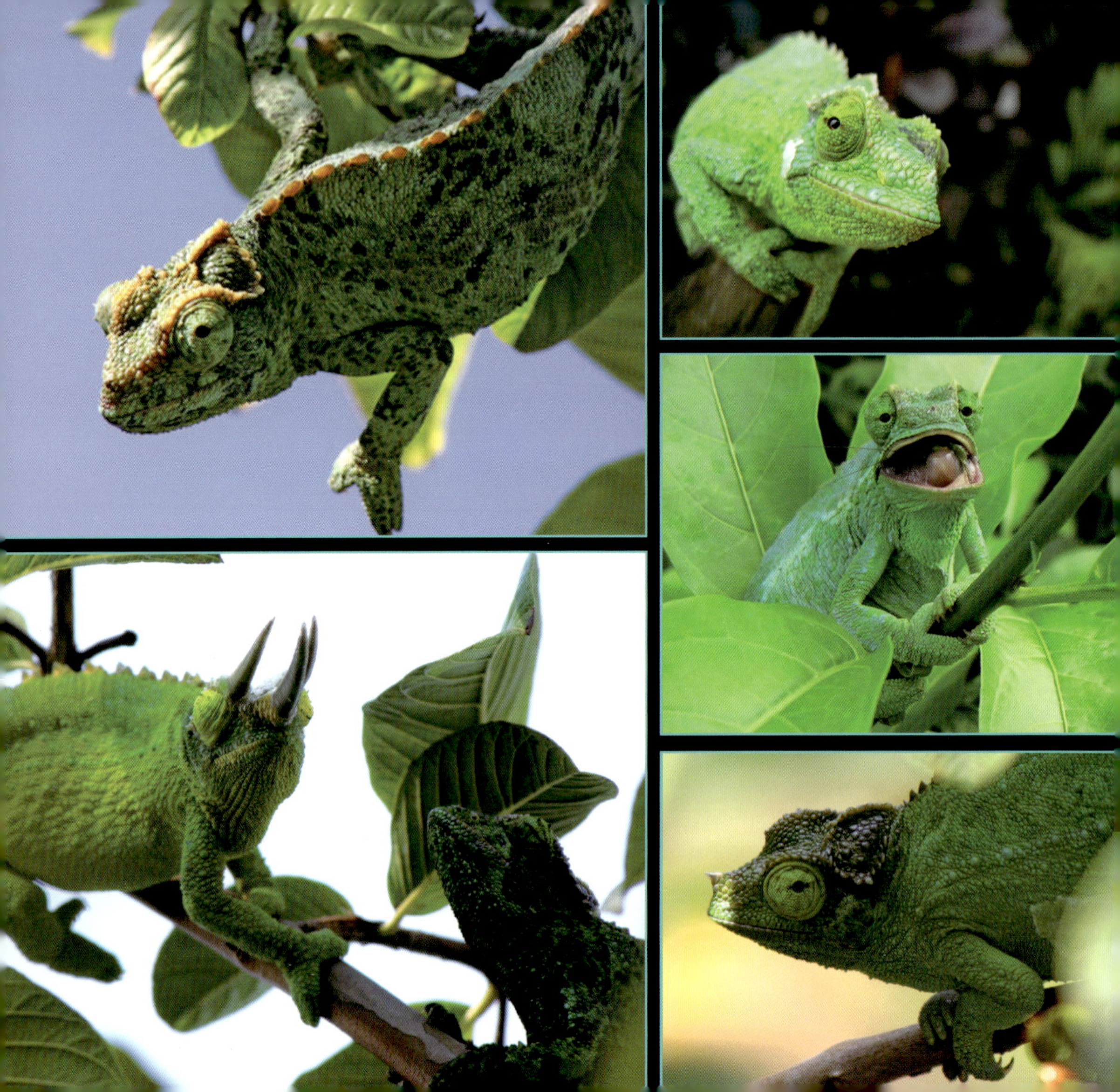

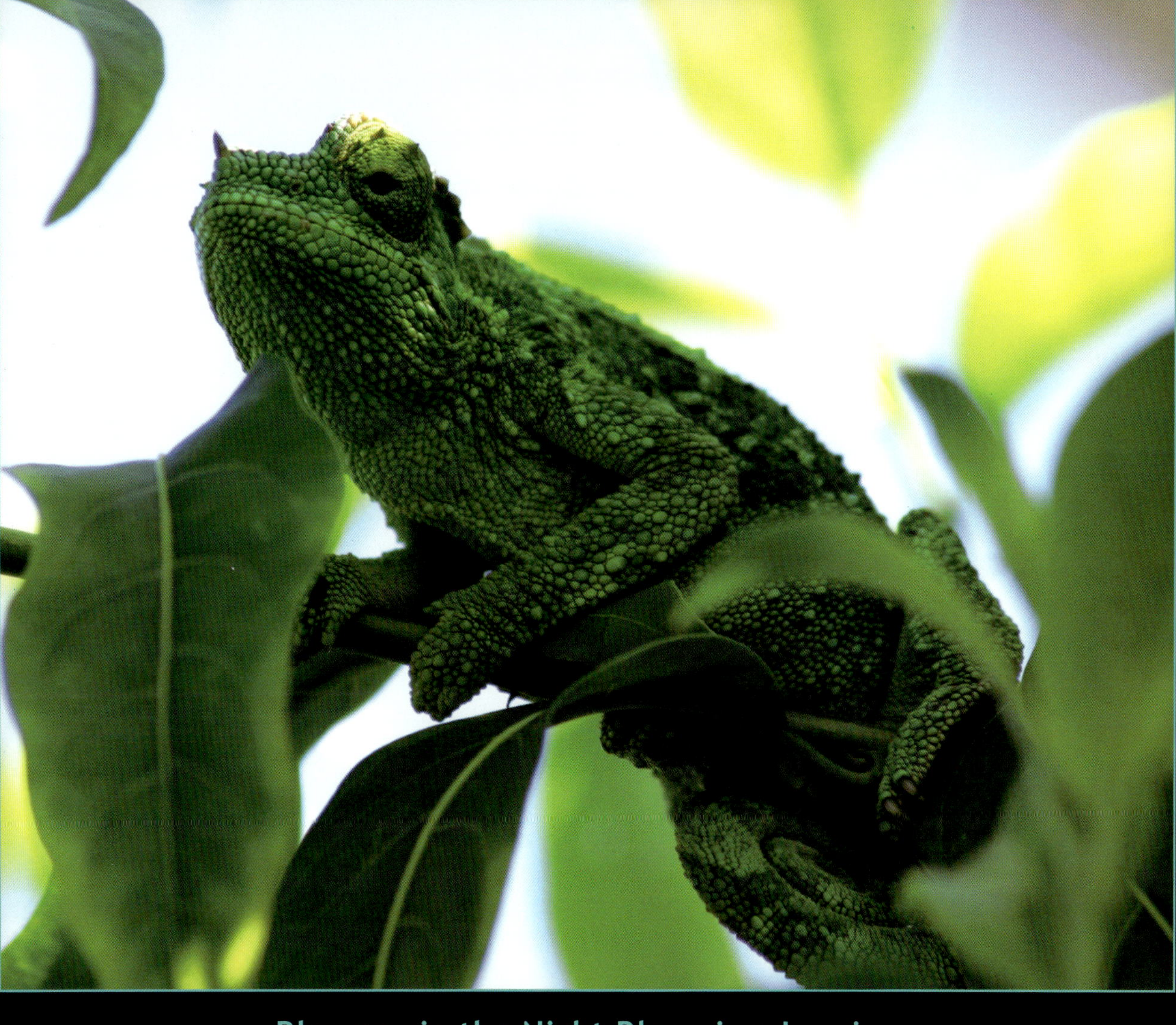

Bloomer in the Night Blooming Jasmine

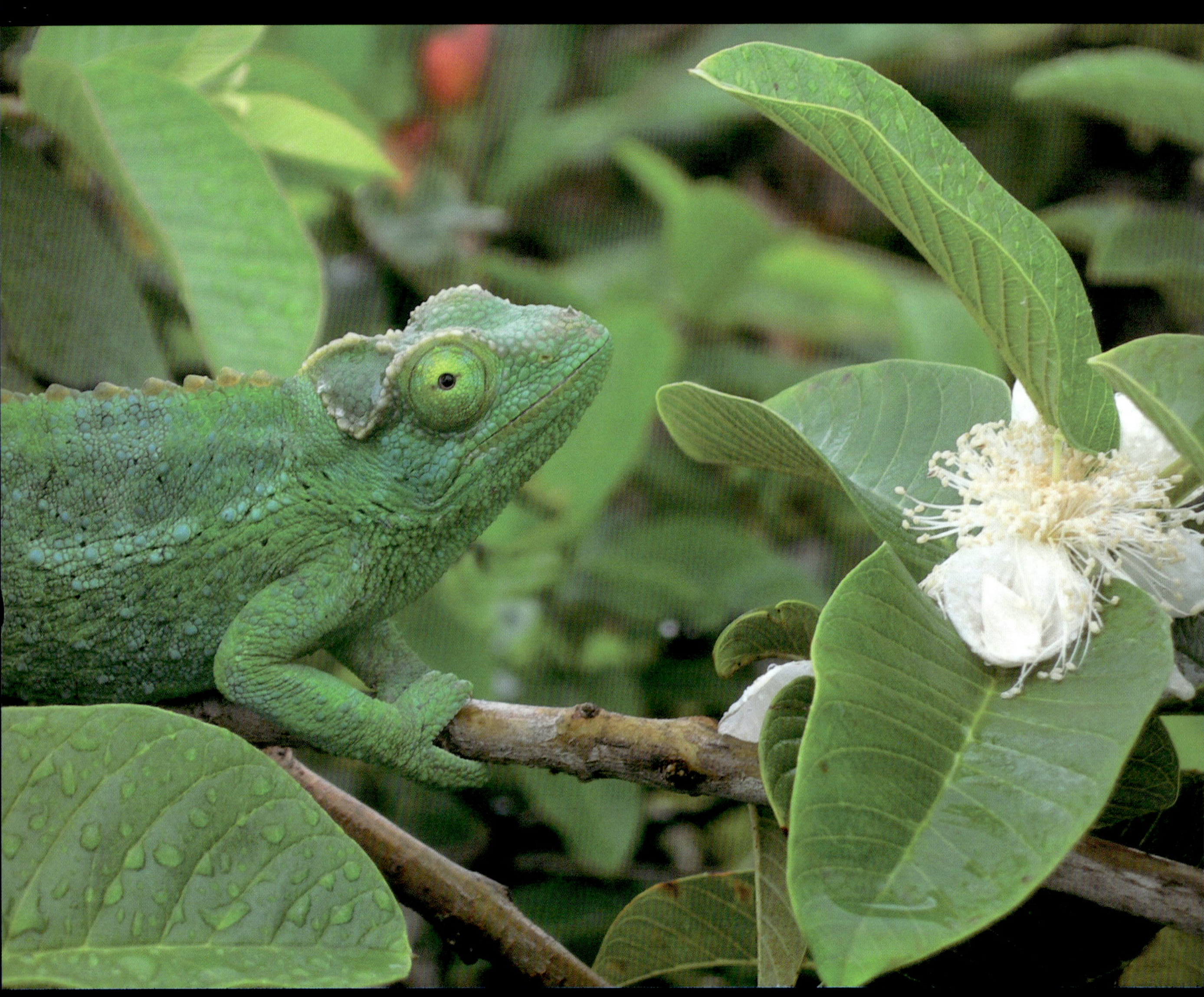

Lulu by a Guava Blossom

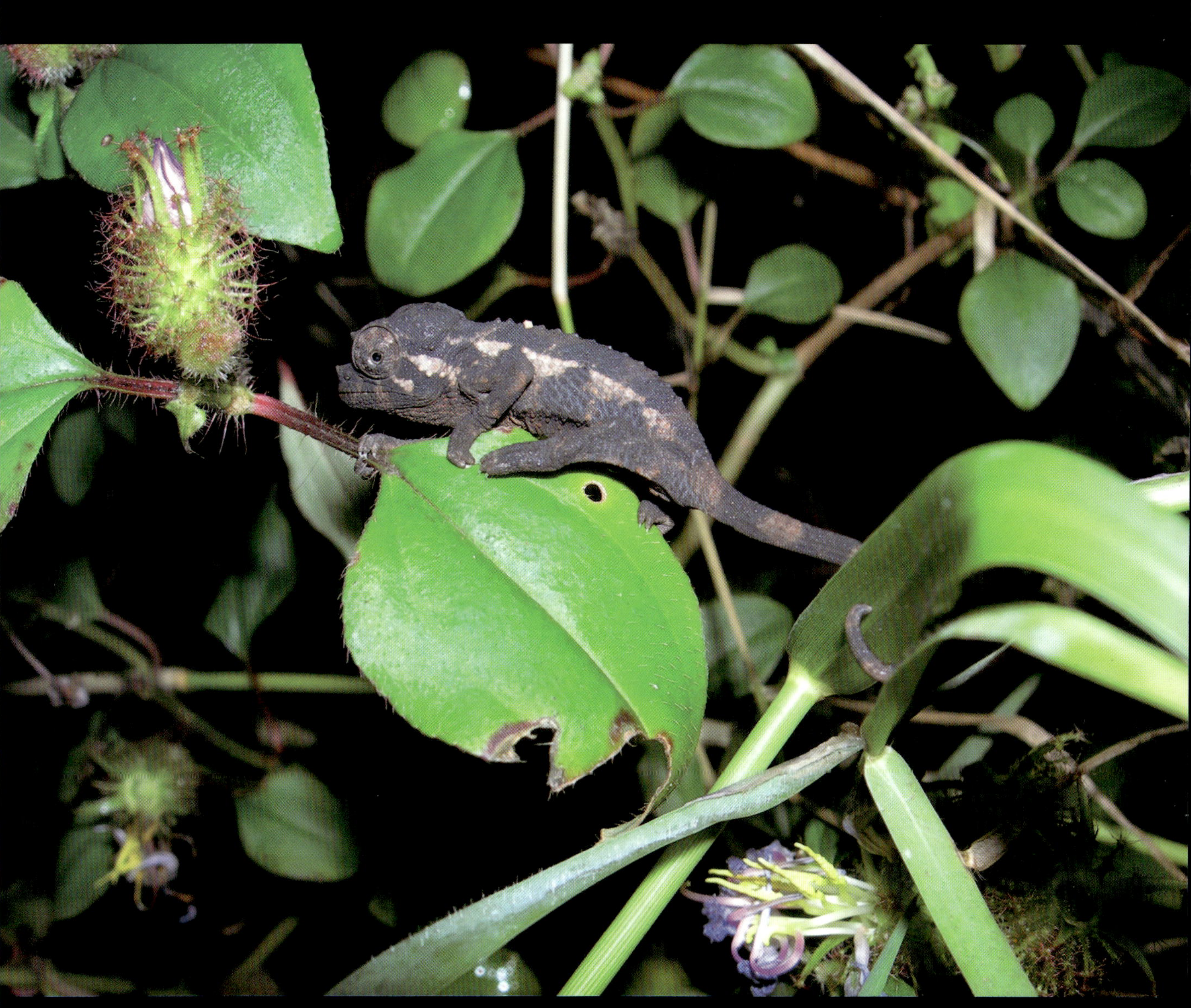

Spider Monkey

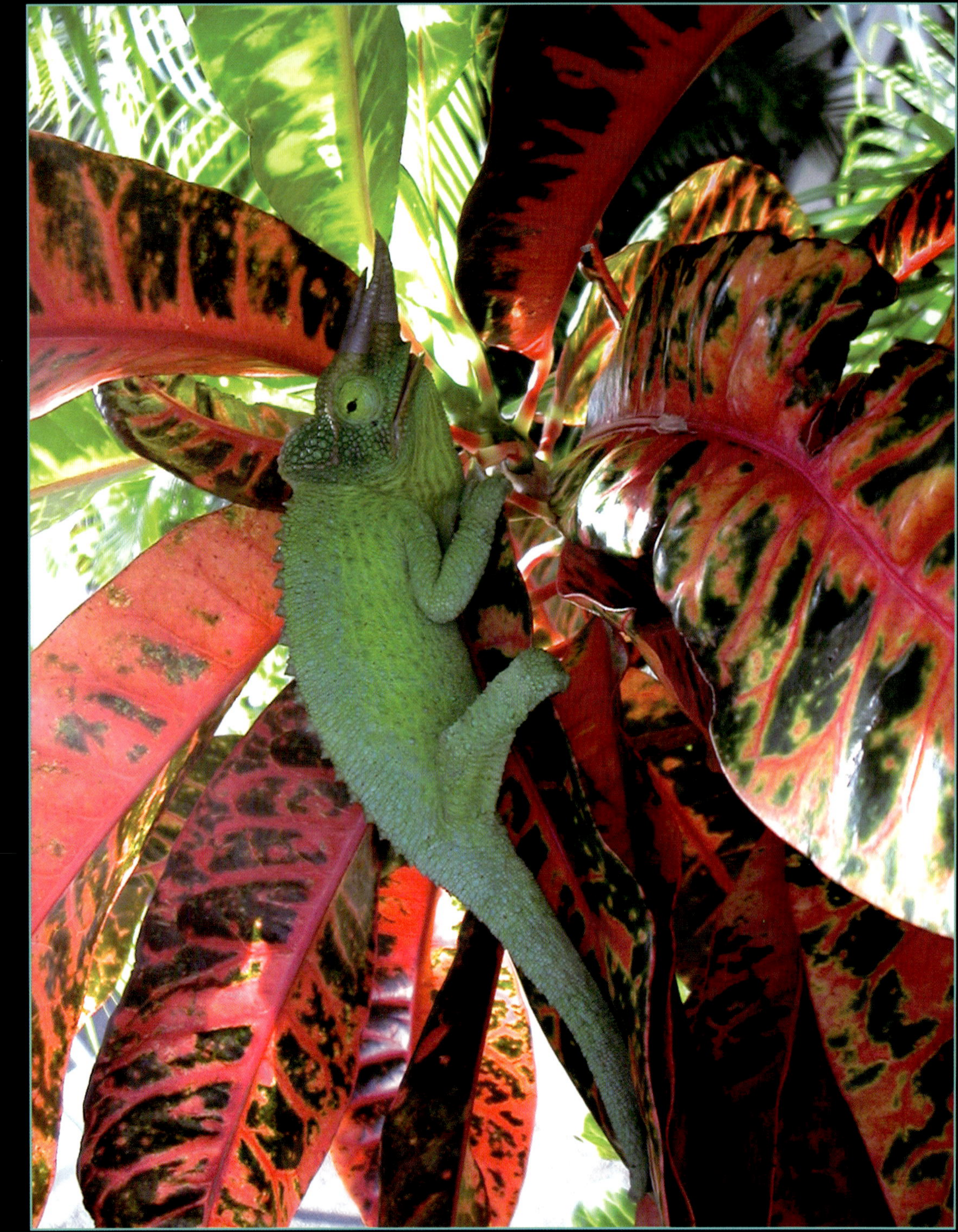

Spike

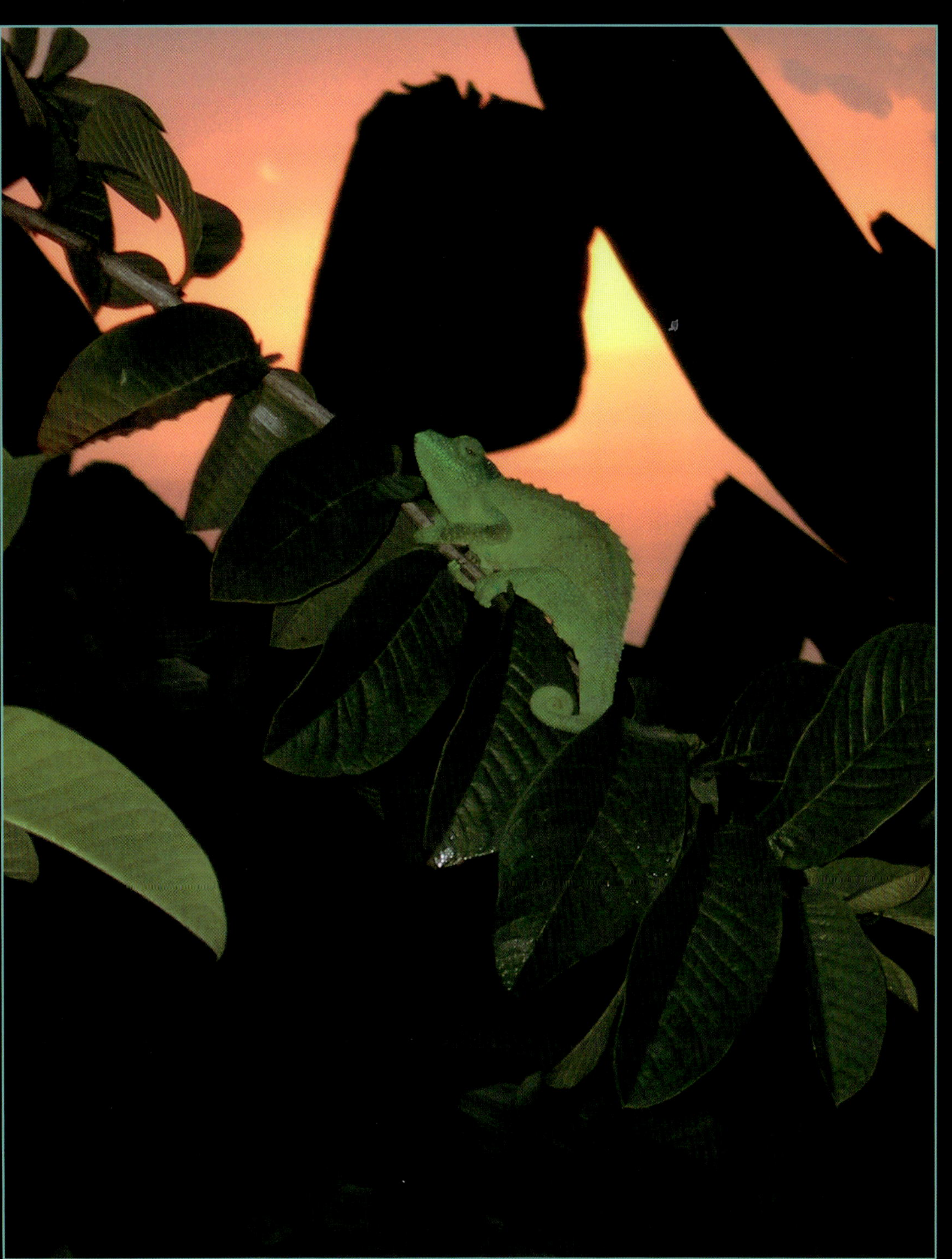

Lulu

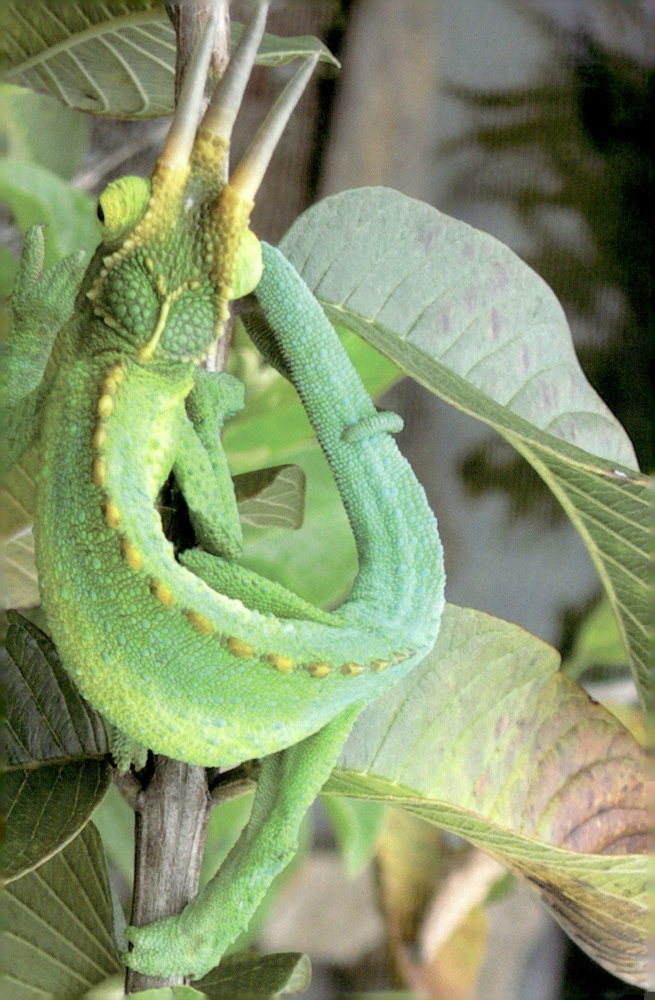

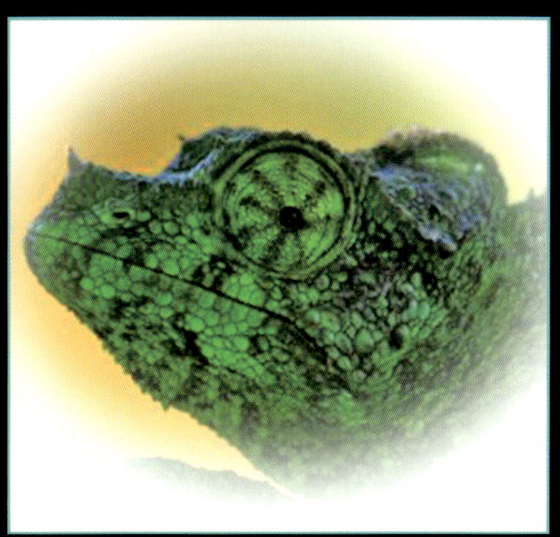

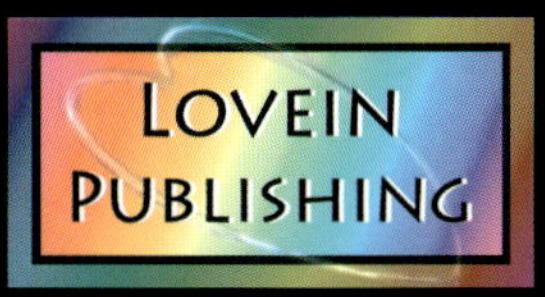

P.O. Box 773, Holualoa Village, Big Island of Hawaii, 96725
www.lovein.com